Science and Religion: A Very Short Introduction

VERY SHORT INTRODUCTIONS are for anyone wanting a stimulating and accessible way into a new subject. They are written by experts, and have been translated into more than 45 different languages.

The series began in 1995, and now covers a wide variety of topics in every discipline. The VSI library currently contains over 700 volumes—a Very Short Introduction to everything from Psychology and Philosophy of Science to American History and Relativity—and continues to grow in every subject area.

Very Short Introductions available now:

Available soon:

For more information visit our website

www.oup.com/vsi/

Thomas Dixon and Adam R. Shapiro

SCIENCE AND RELIGION

A Very Short Introduction

SECOND EDITION

OXFORD
UNIVERSITY PRESS

OXFORD
UNIVERSITY PRESS

Great Clarendon Street, Oxford, OX2 6DP,
United Kingdom

Oxford University Press is a department of the University of Oxford.
It furthers the University's objective of excellence in research, scholarship,
and education by publishing worldwide. Oxford is a registered trade mark of
Oxford University Press in the UK and in certain other countries

First edition published 2008
This edition published 2022

Impression: 1

Published in the United States of America by Oxford University Press
198 Madison Avenue, New York, NY 10016, United States of America

British Library Cataloguing in Publication Data
Data available

Library of Congress Control Number: 2021949066

ISBN 978-0-19-883102-0

Printed in Great Britain by
Ashford Colour Press Ltd, Gosport, Hampshire

For Emma Dixon and Stacey Bhaerman

Contents

Preface

Books about science and religion generally fall into one of two categories: those that want to persuade you of the plausibility of religion and those that want to do the opposite. This *Very Short Introduction* falls into neither category. It aims instead to offer an informative and even-handed account of what is really at stake. The polemical passion the subject often generates is an indication of the intensity with which people identify themselves with their beliefs about nature and God, whether they are religious or not. The origins and functions of those beliefs form the subject of this book.

Historical notions about famous individuals, especially Galileo Galilei and Charles Darwin, philosophical assumptions about miracles, laws of nature, and scientific knowledge, and discussions of the religious and moral implications of modern science, from quantum mechanics to neuroscience, are regular features of science–religion debates today. All of these are scrutinized here. Increasingly, people also recognize that 'science' and 'religion' describe two types of thought that first became separated and compared in European cultures—and that the global story of 'science and religion' is one shaped by legacies of colonialism and cultural contact.

It is not our aim in this book to persuade people to stop disagreeing with each other about science and religion—far from it. Our hope is only that it might help people to disagree with each other in a well-informed way.

Acknowledgements

Thomas Dixon

I remain grateful to all the wonderful scholars, colleagues, and friends I thanked in the first edition of this book, including Fraser Watts, John Hedley Brooke, Janet Browne, Hasok Chang, Rob Iliffe, Jim Moore, Jim Secord, Stephen Pumfrey, Geoffrey Cantor, Colin Jones, Miri Rubin, Virginia Davis, Yossi Rapoport, and the late Peter Lipton. Friends who kindly read the first edition in draft included Emily Butterworth, Noam Friedlander, James Humphreys, Finola Lang, Dan Neidle, Trevor Sather, Léon Turner, and Giles Shilson. The first edition was dedicated to my sister Emma, who—many years ago—advised me to become an academic and not a lawyer, and I remain grateful to her and to my whole family for their support, especially Emily, Caleb, and Laurie. My greatest thanks in this second edition, however, are reserved for my co-author Adam R. Shapiro who has done virtually all the work in improving, updating, and expanding this text and extending its life and usefulness for a new generation of readers. Thank you, Adam!

Adam R. Shapiro

Thomas and I first met in 2007 at the conference on 'Science and Religion: Historical and Contemporary Perspectives' at Lancaster University, which marked John Hedley Brooke's retirement. As a new Ph.D., that conference was one of my first opportunities to connect with science and religion scholars from around the globe. Thomas invited me to contribute to the volume that came from that conference and I am very grateful that over a decade later, he asked me to build upon the excellent work he did in creating the first edition of this text. I am indebted to my mentors, Ron Numbers, Adrian Johns, and Bob Richards. I especially wish to thank Sarah Qidwai and Scott Prinster for discussions with me about recent directions in the study of science and religion and what new questions and topics merited discussion (more than could fit!) Lastly, all thanks to Stacey, Yitzy, and Moti—from whose stolen minutes this book was written.

List of illustrations

The publisher and the authors apologize for any errors or omissions in the above list. If contacted they will be pleased to rectify these at the earliest opportunity.

Chapter 1
What are science–religion debates really about?

In Rome on 22 June 1633 Galileo Galilei went down on his knees. The Inquisition of the Roman Catholic Church had found him 'vehemently suspected of heresy, namely, of having held and believed a doctrine which is false and contrary to the divine and Holy Scripture'. This was the doctrine that 'the sun is the centre of the world and does not move from east to west, that the earth moves and is not the centre of the world, and that one may hold and defend as probable an opinion after it has been declared and defined as contrary to Holy Scripture'. The 70-year-old Florentine philosopher and astronomer was sentenced to imprisonment (later commuted to house arrest) and instructed to recite the seven penitential Psalms once a week for the next three years. His penance included a particularly apt line in Psalm 102: 'In the beginning you laid the foundations of the earth, and the heavens are the work of your hands.' Kneeling before the 'Reverend Lord Cardinals, Inquisitors-General', Galileo accepted his sentence, swore complete obedience to the 'Holy Catholic and Apostolic Church', and declared that he cursed and detested the 'errors and heresies' of which he had been suspected—namely belief in a Sun-centred cosmos and in the movement of the Earth.

According to the mythology that grew around Galileo's trial, after publicly repudiating his beliefs, he supposedly muttered 'E pur si muove' (And yet it moves). There is no proof that Galileo actually said this, but for centuries the Galileo legend has been used to advance a story about science being oppressed by religion. The portrayal of Galileo as the abused martyr who championed empirical truth against the biblical bigotry of organized religion is probably the most famous example of the idea that science and religion are inevitably in conflict. Later episodes of science–religion encounters—debates over the meaning of evolution and the nature of human morality, the origins of the cosmos, even the relationship between human beings and their planetary environment—all take place within the orbit of that Galilean folk tale. Ultimately, Galileo was correct that the Earth does move—it orbits the Sun once a year. But, as we will see, the Inquisition's punishment of Galileo was not the clear-cut case of 'science' versus 'religion' that is often told.

The Victorian agnostic Thomas Huxley expressed this idea of religion battling science vividly in his review of Charles Darwin's *The Origin of Species* (1859). 'Extinguished theologians', Huxley wrote, 'lie about the cradle of every science as the strangled snakes beside that of Hercules; and history records that whenever science and orthodoxy have been fairly opposed, the latter has been forced to retire from the lists, bleeding and crushed if not annihilated; scotched, if not slain.' The image of conflict has also been attractive to some religious believers, who use it to portray themselves as members of an embattled but righteous minority struggling heroically to protect their faith against the oppressive and intolerant forces of science and materialism.

Although the idea of warfare between science and religion remains widespread and popular, most recent academic writing on the subject has undermined this hypothesis of an inevitable conflict. As we shall see, there are good reasons for rejecting simple conflict stories. From Galileo's trial in 17th-century Rome to modern American struggles over acceptance of evolution and human-caused climate change, there has been more to the relationship between science and religion than meets the eye.

Pioneers of early modern science such as Isaac Newton and Robert Boyle saw their study of nature as part of a religious enterprise devoted to understanding God's creation. Galileo too thought that science and religion could exist in mutual harmony. The goal of a constructive and collaborative dialogue between science and religion has been endorsed by members of religious traditions all around the world, as well as many scientists, who continue to see their research as a complement rather than a challenge to their faith.

Does that mean that the story of science and religion is actually one of harmony, rather than conflict? Certainly not. The primary thing to avoid is too narrow an idea of the kinds of conflicts or harmonies one might expect to find between science and religion. Individuals, ideas, and institutions can and have come into conflict, or been resolved into harmony, in an endless array of different combinations.

Historian John Hedley Brooke writes that serious historical study has 'revealed so extraordinarily rich and complex a relationship between science and religion in the past that general theses are difficult to sustain. The real lesson turns out to be the complexity.' That complexity will be explored in subsequent chapters. There has certainly not been a single and unchanging relationship between two entities called 'science' and 'religion'. There are, nonetheless, some central philosophical and political questions that have frequently recurred in this context: What are the most authoritative sources of knowledge? What is the most fundamental reality? What kind of creatures are human beings? What is the proper relationship between church and state? Who should control education? Can either scripture or nature serve as a reliable ethical guide?

Debates about science and religion are, on the face of it, about the intellectual compatibility or incompatibility of some particular religious belief with some particular aspect of scientific knowledge.

3

Does belief in life after death or free will conflict with the findings of modern brain science? Is belief in the Bible incompatible with believing that humans and chimpanzees evolved from a common ancestor? Does belief in miracles conflict with the strictly law-governed world revealed by the physical sciences? One answer to the question that titles this chapter—What are science–religion debates really about?—is that they are about these issues of intellectual compatibility.

What we especially want to emphasize in this *Very Short Introduction*, however, is that these contemporary contests of ideas are the visible tips of much larger and deeper-lying structures. Our aim will be to look historically at how we came to think as we do about science and religion, to explore philosophically what preconceptions about knowledge are involved, and to reflect on the political and ethical questions that often set the unspoken agenda for these intellectual debates. More often than not, questions about science and religion take place in a wider social and cultural context. Often, what science–religion debates are really about is not just finding some abstract truth about human nature or the cosmos, but using those concepts to negotiate issues that affect our daily lives.

Encountering nature

Scientific knowledge is based on observations of the natural world. But observing the natural world is neither as simple nor as solitary an activity as it might sound. Take the Moon, for instance. When you look up at the sky on a clear night, what do you see? You see the Moon and the stars. But what do you actually observe? There are a lot of small bright lights and then a larger whitish circular object. If you had never learned any science, what would you think this white object was? Is it a flat disc, or is it a sphere? If the latter, then why do we always see the same side of it? And why does its shape appear to change from a thin crescent to a full disc and back again? Is it an object like the Earth? If so, how big is it? And how close? And do people live there? Or is it a smaller night-time equivalent of the Sun? Finally, perhaps it is like one of the little bright lights but larger or closer? In any case, how and why does it move across the sky like that? Is something else pushing it or does it move on its own? Is it attached to an invisible mechanism of some kind? Is it a supernatural being?

You might already know that the Moon is a large spherical rocky satellite which orbits the Earth completely about once a month and which rotates once on its own axis in the same time (which explains why we always see the same side of it). You may know that the Moon does not generate its own light, but reflects light from the Sun. The changing relative positions of the Sun, Earth, and Moon explain why the Moon displays 'phases'—with either the entirety or only a small crescent of the illuminated half of the Moon visible at a particular time. You may also know that all physical bodies are attracted to each other by a gravitational force in proportion to the product of their masses and in inverse proportion to the square of the distance between them, and that this helps to explain the regular motions of the Moon around the Earth and of the Earth around the Sun. You will probably also know that the bright little lights in the night sky are stars, similar to our Sun; that the ones visible to the naked eye are thousands of light years away and those observable through telescopes are millions or even billions of light years away; so that to look up at the night sky is to look into the distant past of our universe. But however much of all this you know, you did not find it out by observation alone. You were told it. You possibly learned it from your parents or a science teacher or a television programme or an online encyclopedia. Even professional astronomers will not generally have checked the truth of any of the statements made in this paragraph by their own empirical observations. Astronomers are not lazy or incompetent, but they know that they can rely on the amassed authoritative observations and theoretical reasonings of the scientific community which, over a period of many centuries, have established these facts as fundamental physical truths.

The point is that while it is certainly true that scientific knowledge is based on and tested against observations of the natural world, there is an awful lot more to it than just pointing your sense organs in the right direction. As an individual, even an individual scientist, only the tiniest fraction of what you know is based directly on your own observations. And even then, those observations only make sense within a complex framework of existing facts and theories which have been accumulated and developed through many centuries. You know what you do about the Moon and the stars because of a long and complex cultural history (a small part of which is told in Chapter 2), which mediates between the light from the night sky and your thoughts about astronomy and cosmology. That history includes challenges to the old Earth-centred world-view by Galileo Galilei, made with the help of Copernicus' astronomy and the newly invented telescope in the early 17th century (Figure 1)—as well as the establishment of Newton's laws of motion and gravitation later in that century and more recent developments in physics and cosmology too. It also includes, crucially, the histories of those social and political mechanisms that allow for, and control, the dissemination of scientific knowledge among the people through books and letters and in classrooms and laboratories.

We should also notice, by the way, that what science often aims to show is that things in themselves are not as they initially seem to us—that appearances can be deceptive. The Earth beneath our feet certainly seems to be solid and stable, and the Sun and the other stars appear to move around us. But science eventually showed that, despite all the sensory evidence to the contrary, the Earth is not only spinning on its own axis but is also hurtling around the Sun at great speed. Indeed, one of the characters in Galileo's *Dialogue Concerning the Two Chief World Systems* (1632) expresses admiration for those who, like Aristarchus and Copernicus, had been able to believe in the Sun-centred system before the advent of the telescope: 'I cannot sufficiently admire the intellectual eminence of those who received it and held it to be

1. The Moon as engraved by the artist Claude Mellan from early 17th-century telescopic observations.

true. They have by sheer force of intellect done such violence to their own senses as to prefer what reason told them over that which sense experience plainly showed them to be the case.'
In more recent times, both evolutionary biology and quantum mechanics have similarly required people to believe implausible

things—that we share an ancestor not only with rabbits but also with carrots, for example, or that the smallest components of matter can behave both as waves and as particles. People sometimes say that science is just a systematization of empirical observations, or nothing more than the careful application of common sense. However, it also has the ambition and the potential to show that our senses deceive us and that our basic intuitions may lead us astray.

But when you look up at the night sky, you may not be thinking about data or theories taken from astronomy and cosmology at all. You may instead be gripped by a wider sense of the power of nature, the beauty and grandeur of the heavens, the vastness of space and time, and your own smallness and insignificance. This could even be a spiritual experience for you, reinforcing your feeling of awe at the power of God and the immensity and complexity of creation, bringing to mind the words of Psalm 19: 'The heavens declare the glory of God; the skies proclaim the work of his hands.'

Such an emotional and religious response to the night sky would, of course, be every bit as historically and culturally mediated as the experience of perceiving the Moon and the stars in terms of modern cosmology. Without some kind of religious education you certainly would not be able to quote from the Bible, and you would perhaps not even be able to formulate a developed concept of God. Individual religious experiences, like modern scientific observations, are made possible by long processes of human collaboration in a shared quest for understanding. In the religious case, what intervenes between the light hitting your retina and your thoughts about the glory of God is a lengthy history of a particular set of sacred stories, passed down orally or as texts, and their interpretation within a succession of human communities. And, as in the scientific case, one of the lessons learned through that communal endeavour is that things are not always as they seem. Religious teachers, as much as scientific ones, try to show their pupils that there is an unseen world behind the observed one—and one which might overturn their most settled intuitions and beliefs.

The political dimension

Among historians of science and religion there have been two primary forms of refutation of the 'conflict narrative' favoured by Enlightenment rationalists, Victorian freethinkers, and modern-day scientific atheists. The first strategy is to replace the overarching image of conflict with that of complexity: to put emphasis on the very different ways that science–religion interactions have developed at different times, in different places, and in different local circumstances. Some scientists have been religious, others atheist. Some religious denominations welcome certain aspects of modern science, others are suspicious. Recognizing that neither 'science' nor 'religion' refers to a simple singular entity is an important part of this approach too, as is acknowledging the existence of considerable national and linguistic differences. To take one well-known example, debates about evolution and religion have developed quite differently in the United States from how they have in Europe and elsewhere. As discussed in Chapter 4, the debates about the teaching of evolution in schools are shaped by the legal and political circumstances that affect how education is regulated.

If this first approach to debunking the conflict narrative is to complicate the plot, the second involves recasting the leading characters. This approach says: yes, there have been real conflicts, but they are not clashes between science and religion. The question then is: who or what are the real antagonists in this story? Sometimes, what appears to be a case of science versus religion is actually a case of one religious world-view against another religious world-view, with scientific theories and observations shaping how the two sides debate. In other cases, a local political issue is redescribed by its partisans as a conflict between science and religion to make the fight seem grander, more epic, and morally justified. By associating with the seemingly timeless debate of 'science versus religion', disputants can describe themselves as martyrs, as patriots, or on the right 'side of history'.

There is certainly not a simple recasting that works for all cases, but the general idea is that the real conflict is a political one about the production and dissemination of knowledge. The opposition of science versus religion is then seen to be standing proxy for some classic modern political conflicts: the individual versus the state, or secular liberalism versus conservative traditionalism.

Questions about the politics of knowledge will arise repeatedly in subsequent chapters. For the moment, let us consider just one other example—the philosopher and firebrand Thomas Paine. An unsuccessful corset-maker, sacked tax-collector, and occasional political writer, Paine left his native England to start a new life in America in 1774. A couple of years later, his polemical pamphlet *Common Sense* (1776) was a key factor in persuading the American colonists to go to war against the British government, and established Paine as the best-selling author of the age. An associate of Benjamin Rush, Thomas Jefferson, and other founders of the United States of America, Paine's democratic and anti-monarchical political philosophy shaped the Declaration of Independence. Paine also attended popular lectures on Newton and astronomy back in England, and he spent many years of his life working on a design for a single-span iron bridge, inspired by the delicacy and strength of one of the great works of nature—the spider's web. He saw revolutions in governments paralleling the revolutions of celestial bodies in the heavens. Each was an inevitable, natural, and law-governed process. Later in life, having had a hand in both the American and French revolutions, Paine turned his sights from monarchy to Christianity. The institutions of Christianity were as offensive to his enlightened and Newtonian sensibilities as were those of monarchical government. In his *Age of Reason* (1794), Paine complained of 'the continual persecution carried on by the Church, for several hundred years, against the sciences and against the professors of science'.

Paine's version of the conflict narrative makes most sense when seen in its political context. Paine was a scientific thinker who was opposed to Christianity. He denounced the Bible, especially the Old Testament, with its stories of 'voluptuous debaucheries' among the Israelites and the 'unrelenting vindictiveness' of their God. To the shock of his friends, Paine wrote of the Bible: 'I sincerely detest it, as I detest everything that is cruel.' Paine also lambasted the 'priestcraft' at work in the 'adulterous' relationship between the Church of England and the British state. What he hoped for, though, was not an end to religion but the replacement of Christianity by a rational religion based on the study of nature—one which recognized the existence of God, the importance of morality, and the hope for a future life, but did away with scriptures, priests, and the authority of the state. His reasons for this were democratic ones. National churches lorded illegitimate power over the people by claiming special access to divine truths and revelations. But everyone can read the book of nature and understand the goodness, power, and generosity of its author. In the religion of Deism recommended by Paine, there was no need for the people to be in thrall either to priests or to the state. Science could replace Christianity by showing that every individual could find God by looking at the night sky rather than by reading the Bible or going to church. 'That which is now called natural philosophy', Paine wrote, 'embracing the whole circle of science of which astronomy occupies the chief place, is the study of the works of God, and of the power and wisdom of God and his works, and is the true theology.'

Looking to the laws of nature to explain moral and political philosophy was not only the recourse of radicals; as we will see in Chapter 3, the idea that the book of nature offers moral and political guidance was also embraced by the more conservative William Paley in his *Natural Theology* (1802). Both Paley's vision

11

of religious toleration and Paine's ideals of the separation of church and state are enshrined in the founding documents of the United States. And in modern America, too, it is competing political visions that come into conflict in debates about science and religion. American politicians who cast doubt upon the scientific theories of evolution, human-caused climate change, or public health efforts often do so to send a signal—to indicate their general support for Christianity, their opposition to excessively secularist interpretations of the Constitution, and their hostility to naturalistic and materialistic world-views.

The interplay of science and religion has also been used as a literary device, memorably in two mid-20th-century stage plays inspired by real moments of historical conflict. Bertolt Brecht's *Life of Galileo* was composed during the 1930s and early 1940s. Brecht was a German communist, opposed to fascism, and living in exile in Denmark and subsequently the United States. The play uses the story of Galileo to investigate the dilemmas faced by a dissident intellectual living under a repressive regime, and also to discuss the importance of pursuing scientific knowledge for moral and social ends rather than purely for its own sake. Brecht saw in the well-known Galileo affair political lessons which could be applied to a world struggling against authoritarian fascism and, in the later version of the play, questioning the ethical actions of scientists after the atomic bombing of Hiroshima and Nagasaki.

Jerome Lawrence and Robert E. Lee's play *Inherit the Wind*, first performed in 1955, and made into a famous film in 1960, was a dramatization of the Scopes 'monkey trial' of 1925. The historical events on which the play was based are discussed in Chapter 4. *Inherit the Wind* used Scopes's prosecution for the crime of teaching about evolution to draw connections between the religious bigotry associated with creationism in the United States in the 1920s and racial bigotry at the dawn of the civil rights era. Both Brecht's *Galileo* and Lawrence and Lee's *Inherit the Wind* used the tension between science and religion to explore themes of intellectual freedom, fascism and censorship, political power, and human morality.

'Science and religion' as an academic field

So far we have looked at science and religion as two distinct cultural enterprises which interact in both the personal and political spheres. There is an important further dimension to add to this preliminary picture, which is the development of 'science and religion' as an academic field in its own right.

Of course theologians, philosophers, and scientists have been writing treatises about the relationship between natural knowledge and revelation for centuries. Many of these works were very popular, especially in the 18th and 19th centuries. The *Bridgewater Treatises on the power, wisdom and goodness of God as manifested in the creation* was a series of eight books endowed by the bequest of the Earl of Bridgewater in the 1830s; they became widely read as both works of theology and texts of popular science. Toward the end of the 19th century, Lord Adam Gifford established a lecture series to promote natural theology at four Scottish universities. The Gifford Lectures remain one of the most prominent lecture series about science and religion. However, from the 1950s onwards 'science and religion' took on a more distinct existence as an academic discipline. The Institute on Religion in an Age of Science (IRAS) began its annual meetings at Star Island, New Hampshire, in 1954, and in 1966 the first specialist journal in the field was founded in Chicago—*Zygon: Journal of Religion and Science*. The same year saw the publication of a very widely used textbook, *Issues in Science and Religion* by the British physicist and theologian Ian Barbour. Since that time, various organizations have fostered this kind of work, including a European Society for the Study of Science and Theology, and an International Society for Science and Religion. There are established academic chairs and research centres devoted specifically to the study of science and religion at many major universities around the world.

Academic work by scientists and theologians seeking to develop a harmonious interdisciplinary dialogue has been supported by a range of institutions, including the Roman Catholic Church, through the work of the Vatican Observatory, and also the John Templeton Foundation in America—a philanthropic organization particularly committed to supporting research that harmonizes science with religion. The Templeton Foundation spends millions of dollars on research grants each year, including an annual Templeton Prize, currently valued at about $1.5 million, given to 'a living person who has made an exceptional contribution to affirming life's spiritual dimension'. Former winners have included scientists, and leaders of several world religions, as well as individuals who have contributed to the academic dialogue between science and religion. They include St Teresa of Kolkata (Mother Teresa), *Zygon* journal founder Ralph Wendell Burhoe, Nobel-winning physicist Charles Townes, the Tibetan Buddhist leader the Dalai Lama, and the anthropologist Jane Goodall. As with many other elite awards, including the Nobel prizes in the sciences, Templeton Prize recipients have disproportionately been men. Many Templeton prizewinners—along with others who have contributed to the creation of 'science and religion' as an academic subject—fall into the category of religiously committed professional scientists (and in some cases ordained ministers). There are also many historians, philosophers, and theologians who have contributed significantly to the field.

Whether arguing for conflict or for harmony, it could be objected that any academic field addressing 'the relationship between science and religion' obscures the true plurality and complexity of the terms. 'Science' and 'religion' are both hazy categories with blurry boundaries and long histories. And different sciences and different religions have clearly related to each other in a variety of ways. Mathematics and astronomy were both particularly nurtured in Islamic societies, for example. In the Middle Ages they were used to calculate the correct times of prayer and the direction of Mecca, as well as for other, more secular, purposes. Muslim scholars working in academies such as the House of Wisdom in Baghdad preserved, tested, and improved upon ancient Greek medicine and optics, as well as astronomy and astrology, between the 9th and the 15th centuries. The motto of these scholars was: 'Whoever does not know astronomy and anatomy is deficient in the knowledge of God.' Their works were also crucial sources for the revival of European learning from the later Middle Ages onwards.

Historically excluded from more mainstream European academic institutions, Jewish communities formed a particularly strong connection with sciences and medicine in early modern Europe. The Roman Catholic Church, despite the high-profile difficulties caused by Galileo's ideas, was one of the largest sponsors of scientific research during the 16th and 17th centuries, especially through the investment of the Jesuit order in astronomical observatories and experimental equipment.

'Science' and 'religion' are terms whose definitions and distinctions emerged primarily in Christian European contexts, and yet questions of modern science–religion 'relationships' have been exported to other cultures, languages, and world regions, with nuances often lost in translation. Here we might consider Buddhist neuroscientific studies of the state of the brain during meditation, the 2009 Hindu Declaration on Climate Change, or even Fritjof Capra's 1975 best-seller, *The Tao of Physics: An Exploration of the Parallels between Modern Physics and Eastern Mysticism*. In much of the world, concepts of religion and science—and a relationship between them—are strongly influenced by centuries of colonial and post-colonial history, and the role that sciences, technology, and religions played in creating and governing imperial territories.

In this book, therefore, we examine the phenomenon of 'science and religion' while acknowledging that the phrase, and the ways of thinking it describes, are not as universal as some of its users imagine. In this book, as in many contributions to the field, the 'religions' under discussion are primarily the Abrahamic monotheistic religions of Christianity, Islam, and Judaism. There are good historical reasons for this emphasis, as it is in the European Christian context that 'science' first emerged. These three monotheisms have shared intellectual histories, including the common view that God is the author of two 'books'—the book of nature and the book of scripture—and that the individual believer will find their understanding and their faith strengthened through the careful reading of both books. The intellectual, political, and ethical implications of that shared commitment to reading God's words and works have developed in comparable, although far from identical, ways in these monotheistic traditions. Many other religions and parts of the world beyond Europe first encountered 'science and religion' as part of the cultural exchanges wrought by Western colonialism. To resist using the word 'science' to describe empirical knowledge about nature in the precolonial non-European world is not intended to belittle that knowledge. On the contrary, it is a recognition that science is something specific, contextual, and limited in scope.

No single example of these relationships can serve as a universal template for understanding engagements between science and religion. Some think that the extent of oversimplification, generalization, and reification involved in even using the phrase 'science and religion' makes it a non-starter as a sensible topic. But there is no denying that 'science and religion' has been a topic of academic and popular discussion for well over a century. The fact that the phrase names an academic field, as well as conjuring up vivid if historically debatable cultural stereotypes, justifies its continued use as a category of thought (and as the title of this and many other books). Academics and journalists alike continue to write as if there were some ongoing general relationship between science and religion, in terms of which particular contemporary episodes might be understood. Even if that relationship really exists only in our imaginations, it is still important to try to understand how it got there. Since Galileo Galilei and his encounter with the Roman Inquisition takes centre stage in many popular accounts of that relationship, his story is an appropriate place to start our enquiry.

Chapter 2
Galileo and the philosophy of science

When Galileo recanted his belief that the Earth moved around the Sun, what did that signify? Was it a victory for biblical Christianity and a defeat for scientific rationality? Was it evidence that science and religion are irreconcilable? Nothing so simple. On all sides of the Galileo case, people agreed that it was proper and rational to seek accurate knowledge of the world through both the observation of nature and the revelations recounted in the Bible. The conflict was not between science and religion but rather between differing views within the Catholic Church about how to interpret nature and scripture.

Nicolaus Copernicus had argued for a Sun-centred astronomy in his book *On the Revolutions of the Heavenly Spheres* long before, in 1543. Galileo's observations of the heavens, his writings about the Copernican system, and his trial, all took place in a different political context. An appreciation of the circumstances of Galileo's trial, the shadow cast over it by the Protestant Reformation, and a century of religious warfare, along with the politics of the papal court at the time, all help to explain how these issues took on the dramatic character that they did in 1633, almost a century after Copernicus.

Before considering the Galileo story as a disagreement among 17th-century Catholics about how to read the Bible, it will be useful to look at some general questions about sources of knowledge. These will help to make sense both of what was at stake in Rome in June 1633 and also of general questions about the philosophy of science that still come up in debates about science and religion.

How do we know anything?

We generally derive knowledge of the world from four sources: our senses, our powers of rational thought, the testimony of others, and our memory. All of these sources are fallible. Our senses can deceive us, our reasoning can be faulty, people can knowingly or accidentally mislead us, and most of us know only too well how partial and distorted our memories can be. The whole project of modern science could be summarized as the attempt to weave these individually relatively feeble threads into a more resilient web of knowledge. So the sense experiences of one person must be witnessed, corroborated, and repeated by many others before being accepted as empirical facts. Observations must be supplemented by carefully designed experiments which test more precisely how things behave under different circumstances. Human powers of perception may be limited, but the inventions of the telescope and the microscope in the early 17th century, and of many other sophisticated devices since then, has enormously increased the scope and accuracy of the observations and measurements that are possible. But experiments could not be designed, nor could observations be interpreted, without the use of reason. Theoretical hypotheses about the nature of reality, and reasoning about what experimental evidence is needed to support or refute them, are prerequisites of scientific knowledge.

Finally, scientific experts must cite the sources of their knowledge and explain their chain of reasoning if their testimony is to be accepted. And the publication of scientific results in treatises, books, specialist journals, and electronic databases provides us with a collective and well-documented memory greater than anything that would be possible by relying on one person's memory alone. The knowledge thus produced is a highly prized possession in human societies. It bestows on us the ability to understand and manipulate not only the natural world but also each other. One of the most important advocates of science in 17th-century England, Francis Bacon, wrote that 'human knowledge and human power meet in one; for where the cause is not known the effect cannot be produced'. In other words, an understanding of the secret workings of nature would allow people to produce machines and medicines to improve the human condition. Bacon also wrote, to justify the new knowledge of the period, that 'all knowledge appeareth to be a plant of God's own planting', whose spread and flourishing at that time had been divinely ordained.

Natural philosophers in 17th-century England such as Robert Boyle and Robert Hooke—the new 'virtuosi' of the experimental method, the founders of the Royal Society of London—were perceived by some as a threat to orthodoxy. Their claims to be able both to discover and to manipulate the laws that govern nature seemed to verge on usurping the role of God. That was why it was important to reassure their readers that in reaping this knowledge they were collecting a harvest which was, in Bacon's words, 'of God's own planting'. In this image, God planted the seed of knowledge and natural philosophers harvested its fruit. This agricultural language draws attention to the fact that human knowledge (at least of the natural kind) is cultivated rather than simply found. Seeds do not become plants and bear fruit unless they are sown in proper conditions, are watered and fed, and are harvested in the right way.

In another popular metaphor, God is imagined not as a cosmic planter, but as the author of two books—the book of nature and the book of scripture. This metaphor describes the same idea—that the ultimate source of truth was God and that humans had to adopt certain techniques to acquire knowledge of that truth. Texts do not generally have obvious meanings, but rather these must be teased out through the collective efforts of many readers using different historical and literary techniques. Even if one decides to approach a text in search of its 'literal' meaning, that is by no means a simple matter. It is well known among literary scholars that the project of discerning an author's intentions in a text is a difficult and controversial one. The histories of science and religion reveal that these difficulties have been experienced in full measure in relation to both of God's books. Neither nature nor scripture offers a transparent account of its author's intentions.

This brings us to the question of whether—in addition to sense, reason, testimony, and memory—a fifth source of knowledge needs to be added, namely revelation. It is a belief shared by many Jews, Christians, and Muslims that the natural world reveals the power, intelligence, and goodness of the Creator and that holy scriptures reveal God's plans and the legal and moral basis according to which people should live. Even believing that a scripture is a revealed text does not make the intentions of the divine author immediately transparent, however. Many within religious traditions suggest that it takes years of study, devotion, and perhaps even divine guidance to come to know the meanings of the scriptures.

Natural knowledge is produced by the human powers of sense and rational thought (these faculties can be applied to scripture as well as about the natural world). Moreover, natural knowledge is reproducible and public—you'd expect other reasonable people to reach the same conclusions you do based on their own senses and rational thought. Revealed knowledge is produced by a supernatural uncovering of the truth—either through a divinely inspired scripture or by a direct revelation—a vision or other miraculous experience. Revealed knowledge is more likely to be individual and private. You would not necessarily expect others to reach the same knowledge that you have just because they had gone through the same actions that you did (such as praying while reading a particular passage of scripture).

The private and subjective nature of some supernatural experiences has led philosophers and theologians to seek a more rational and public way of discussing them. *Natural theology*, as opposed to revealed theology, is such a form of discourse—producing ideas about God based on sense and human reason rather than on revelation. This includes theological works making inferences about God from the design apparent in the natural world—as in William Paley's famous *Natural Theology* (1802)—but it also includes other philosophical works about God's existence and attributes. As we shall see, theologians like Paley thought that complete understanding of God was only possible through bringing together both natural and revealed religion.

Debates over science and religion often involve disagreements about the relative authority of different sources of knowledge, and those debates reflect the larger politics of authority and knowledge in society. Thomas Paine's objection to Christian philosophers was not that they found God in nature—he did too—but that they thought they could also find God in the supernatural revelation of the Bible. For Paine, the only possible kind of revelation was from God directly to an individual. If God ever did act in this way, it was revelation 'to the first person only, and hearsay to every other'. The scriptures were therefore nothing more than mere human testimony—second-hand memories—of an alleged revelation and the rational reader was not obliged to believe them. Some advocates of creationism in the 20th and 21st centuries argue that both 'God's word' and 'human reason' are legitimate sources of knowledge, but that the second must always be subordinate to the first, since revealed knowledge is certain while natural knowledge is fallible. While rationalists have rejected revelation altogether, and fundamentalists have insisted that all forms of knowledge be tested against the Bible, many more have looked for ways to reconcile their readings of God's two books without doing violence to either.

The rise and fall of Galileo

Galileo belonged to this last category of believers—seeking harmony between the Bible and knowledge of nature. He endorsed the view that the Bible is about how one goes to heaven and not about how the heavens go. In other words, if you wanted to know about matters pertaining to salvation you should consult scripture, but if you were interested in the detailed workings of the natural world, then there were better starting points—namely empirical observations and reasoned demonstrations. This was not a particularly unorthodox view in itself, but Galileo failed to persuade the authorities that it was a principle that could be applied to his case. The church was certainly not opposed to the study of mathematics, astronomy, and the other sciences. But Galileo didn't limit himself to the book of nature; his writings openly challenged biblical interpretations that were authorized by the church. To the extent that we can distinguish between them, it was his religious claims, not his scientific ones, that drew the attention of the Inquisition.

At the beginning of the 17th century, Galileo was among a tiny handful of natural philosophers who thought it likely that the Copernican astronomy accurately described the universe. The majority of those who took an interest in such questions, including the mathematicians and astronomers working within the Catholic Church, held to the system of physics and cosmology associated with the ancient Greek philosopher Aristotle. There were two elements in this Aristotelian science which were challenged by Galileo. First, there was the Earth-centred model of the cosmos produced by the 2nd-century Greek astronomer Ptolemy. This was the standard model and, despite certain complexities and technical problems, it worked as well as the Copernican model as a device for calculating the positions of the stars and planets, and had the considerable advantage of according with the common-sense intuition that the Earth was not in motion. The second Aristotelian principle that would come under attack was the division of the cosmos into two regions—the sublunary and the superlunary. The sublunary region consisted of everything within the orbit of the Moon. This was the region of corruption and imperfection and of the four elements of earth, water, air, and fire. In the superlunary region, the domain of all the celestial bodies, everything was composed of a fifth element, ether, and was characterized by perfect circular motion (Figure 2).

2. A 16th-century illustration of Ptolemy's Earth-centred astronomical system. At the centre is the world, composed of the four elements of earth, water, air, and fire, surrounded by the spheres of the Moon, Mercury, Venus, the Sun, Mars, Jupiter, Saturn, and finally the sphere of the fixed stars.

Galileo's first contribution to astronomy came when he made use of a recent invention—the 'telescope'. After learning of Dutch telescopes used primarily for distant viewing on land and sea, Galileo built one with improved magnifying power and turned it upwards to observe the sky. The spectacular results were published in two books, *The Starry Messenger* in 1610 and *Letters on Sunspots* in 1613, which established Galileo's reputation as a brilliant observational astronomer and one of the leading natural philosophers in Europe. These works also made it clear that Galileo favoured the Copernican hypothesis.

Just a couple of examples will give a sense of how Galileo wielded his telescope against Aristotelian science. Perhaps the most telling discovery made by Galileo was that Venus, when viewed through the telescope, could be seen to display phases, like the Moon. Its apparent shape varied between a small crescent and a full disc. This strongly suggested that Venus orbited the Sun. In the Ptolemaic system Venus, which was known always to be close to the Sun in the sky, should have appeared always as a thin crescent. Secondly, Galileo was able to deploy a number of key observations against Aristotelian division of the cosmos into distinct sublunary and superlunary regions. His telescope revealed that the Moon was a rocky satellite with craters and mountains—more like the Earth than like an ethereal and perfect heavenly body. He also discovered four satellites or moons orbiting Jupiter. This helped defeat a common objection to the Copernican theory. In the Ptolemaic theory, the Earth's Moon was treated as the closest of several planets, all of whose orbits centred on the Earth. If Copernicus were right, then the Moon would have to orbit the Earth, while the Earth in turn went around the Sun. Was it possible that a celestial body could move in an orbit with a centre other than the centre of the cosmos? The discovery that Jupiter was accompanied in its orbit (whether that was around the Earth or around the Sun) by four satellites established that such motion was indeed possible. Finally, Galileo's discovery of sunspots further undermined the Aristotelian distinction between perfect heavenly bodies and a changeable and imperfect Earth.

Galileo's publications made Copernicanism a live issue in the 1610s. Galileo knew that his advocacy of the new astronomy was arousing both theological and naturalistic objections. One of the reasons for the former was the apparent inconsistency between Copernican astronomy and the Bible. Several passages refer to the Sun moving through the heavens. An often-quoted passage from the Book of Joshua described God stopping the Sun and Moon in the sky. Seeking to pre-empt biblical objections to the view that the Earth moves, in 1615 Galileo wrote his *Letter to the Grand Duchess Christina*, in which he articulated his views about how to deal with apparent conflicts between natural and revealed knowledge. Galileo relied heavily on the views of the Fathers of the Catholic Church, especially St Augustine's idea of the principle of accommodation. This stated that the Bible was written in language accommodated to the limited knowledge of the relatively uneducated people to whom it was initially revealed. Since the first readers of the Book of Joshua believed that the Earth was stationary and the Sun moved around it, God's word was couched in terms that they would understand. Other biblical references to God's 'right hand' or to God's experience of human passions such as anger were generally understood not as literal, but as accommodations to common understanding. Galileo argued that the same attitude should be taken to biblical passages referring to the movement of the Sun. The other principle Galileo adopted was that the Bible should only be given priority in matters relating to salvation. In matters of natural knowledge, if interpretations of scripture seemed to contradict the best available science, then the text would need to be reinterpreted.

All of this was in tune with St Augustine's 4th-century approach to scripture. However, church doctrine about the interpretation of the Bible had now evolved and been more sharply enforced in response to the Protestant Reformation, which continued to divide Europe both politically and religiously throughout the 17th century. One of the central tenets of Protestant forms of Christianity was the right of individuals to read and interpret the Bible for themselves, and in their own language, in contrast to Catholic views that biblical reading required special mental and spiritual training and the sanction of the church. The Catholic Church's principal response to the Reformation came in the form of a series of meetings which comprised the Council of Trent (1545–63). One of the declarations of that Council was that, in matters of faith and morals,

> no one, relying on his own judgement and distorting the Sacred
> Scriptures according to his own conceptions, shall dare to interpret
> them contrary to that sense which Holy Mother Church, to whom it
> belongs to judge their true sense and meaning, has held and does
> hold, or even contrary to the unanimous agreement of the Fathers.

In the context of these Counter-Reformation teachings, Galileo's suggestion in his *Letter to the Grand Duchess Christina* that he, an individual layman, had the authority to tell the 'Holy Mother Church' that his astronomical results required scripture to be reinterpreted smacked both of arrogance and of dangerous Protestant leanings. The fact that in 1632 he would publish his *Dialogue* in vernacular Italian rather than scholarly Latin would add further to that impression.

When a committee was asked to report on the question of Copernicanism to the Inquisition in 1616, it declared it to be both false and absurd as scientific doctrine, and additionally to be contrary to the teachings of scripture and thus formally heretical. Galileo was personally summoned into the presence of Cardinal Robert Bellarmine, who instructed him that he must not hold or defend the Copernican astronomy. At the same time, Copernicus' *On the Revolutions of the Heavenly Spheres*, which had been largely ignored since its appearance in print, was now suspended from publication, pending 'correction'.

The election in 1623 of Cardinal Maffeo Barberini as Pope Urban VIII must have seemed like the answer to Galileo's prayers. Barberini was an educated and cultured Florentine. Since 1611 he had been an admirer and supporter of Galileo's work, even composing a poem, *Adulatio Perniciosa* ('In Dangerous Adulation'), in 1620, expressing admiration for Galileo's telescopic discoveries. In 1624, Galileo had several meetings with Urban VIII, who assured him he could discuss the Copernican theory in his work but only as one hypothesis among others. Urban argued that God, in his omnipotence, could make the heavens move in any way he wished, and so it would be presumptuous to claim to have discovered the precise manner in which this end was achieved. Galileo left Rome reassured and was soon at work on the book that would be published in 1632 as his *Dialogue Concerning the Two Chief World Systems*.

This was when the real trouble started. Although the *Dialogue* was presented as an even-handed discussion among three characters—an Aristotelian, a Copernican, and a common-sensical everyman—it was perfectly clear to most readers that the arguments given in favour of the Copernican system were much stronger than those defending Earth-centred astronomy, and that Galileo had in effect produced Copernican propaganda, thus breaching the conditions of the 1616 injunction and the instructions given by Urban in 1624. That was not all. The Aristotelian character was named 'Simplicio'. This was the name of a 6th-century Aristotelian philosopher but also suggested simple-mindedness. Even more provocatively, one of the arguments put forward by simple Simplicio was the one that had been put to Galileo by Urban himself in 1624—that God could have produced natural effects in any way he chose, and so it was wrong to claim necessary truth for any given physical hypothesis about their causation. This apparent mockery of the Pope added personal insult to the already grave injury delivered by Galileo's disobedience. And the timing could not have been worse. The *Dialogue* reached Rome in 1632 at a moment of great political crisis.

Urban was in the midst of switching his allegiance from the French to the Spanish during the Thirty Years War and was in no mood for leniency. He needed to show his new conservative allies that he was a decisive and authoritative defender of the faith. So Galileo was summoned to Rome to be tried before the Inquisition.

As with the Scopes trial in America three centuries later, the trial of Galileo in 1633 was one in which the outcome was never in doubt. Galileo was found guilty of promoting the heretical Copernican view in contravention of the express injunction not to do so that he had received in 1616. It was for disobeying the church, rather than for seeking to understand the natural world through observation and reasoning, that Galileo was condemned. Galileo's political misjudgement of his relationship with Pope Urban VIII played as much of a role in his downfall as did his overreaching of himself in the field of biblical interpretation. Galileo's work was to be one key contribution to the eventual success of the Copernican theory, which, when modified by further scientific insights such as Kepler's replacement of circular by elliptical orbits, and Newton's discovery of the law of gravitation, was virtually universally accepted. However, in 1632 there was sufficient doubt about the relative merits of the Copernican system and the alternatives (including Tycho Brahe's compromise according to which the Sun orbited the Earth but all the other planets orbited the Sun) that an objective observer would have pronounced the scientific question an open one, making it even harder to decide how to judge between the teachings that the church declared to be contained in the book of scripture and those which Galileo had read through his telescope in the book of nature.

Appearance and reality

The Galileo affair, remembered by some as a clash between science and religion, was primarily a dispute about the enduring political question of who was authorized to produce and disseminate knowledge. In the world of Counter-Reformation

Rome, in the midst of the Thirty Years War, which continued to pit the Protestant and Catholic powers of Europe against each other, Galileo's claim to be able to settle questions about competing sources of knowledge through his own individual reading and reasoning seemed the height of presumption, theologically naive, and a direct threat to the authority of the Church.

The case can also be used to illustrate one further philosophical question that has been central to modern debates about science and religion, namely the issue of *realism*. Arguments about realism particularly arise in connection with what scientific theories have to say about unobservable entities such as magnetic fields, black holes, electrons, quarks, superstrings, and the like. To be a realist is to suppose that science is in the business of providing accurate descriptions of such entities. The anti-realist position is to remain agnostic about the ultimate truth of such descriptions and to hold that science is in the business only of providing accurate predictions of observable phenomena. Urban VIII was not alone among theologians and philosophers in the 16th and 17th centuries in taking an anti-realist or 'instrumentalist' approach to astronomy. On that view, the Ptolemaic and Copernican systems could be used to calculate and predict the apparent motions of the stars and planets, but there was no way to know which system, if either, represented the actual way that God had chosen to structure the heavens. Indeed, when Copernicus' *On the Revolutions of the Heavenly Spheres* was first published, it included a preface written by the Lutheran Andreas Osiander stating that the theory was intended purely as a calculating device rather than as a physical description. Galileo, on the other hand, took a realist attitude, extending it to include the religious claim that his observations explained the way God had made the world. It was his insistence on arguing this which resulted in his trial before the Inquisition.

Galileo was a member of one of the earliest scientific societies, the Academy of Lynxes, founded in 1603 by Prince Cesi. The lynx was thought to see in the dark and so to perceive things invisible to others. Using new scientific instruments such as the telescope and the microscope in conjunction with the power of reason and the language of mathematics, Galileo and his fellow 'lynxes' aimed not just to find useful models for predicting observable phenomena but explanations of those phenomena in terms of the invisible structures and forces of the universe. They seemed to be succeeding. In addition to Galileo's telescopic and astronomical discoveries, the microscope was opening up a different kind of previously unseen world. Using an instrument sent to him by Galileo, Prince Cesi made the first known microscopic observations in the 1620s. Cesi's observations of bees were recorded in engravings by Francesco Stelluti and used as a device to seek approval for the Academy of Lynxes from Urban VIII, whose family coat of arms featured three large bees (Figure 3).

Debates between realists and anti-realists continue to form a lively and fascinating part of the philosophy of science. Each side rests on a very plausible intuition. The realist intuition is that our sense impressions are caused by an external world that exists and has properties independently of human observers, so that it is reasonable to try to discover what those properties are, whether the entities in question are directly observable by us or not. The anti-realist intuition is that all we ever discover, either individually or collectively, is how the world appears to us. We live in an endless series of mental impressions, which we can never compare with the nature of things in themselves. We cannot, even for an instant, draw back the veil of phenomena to check whether our descriptions of reality are right. We can have no knowledge of the world beyond the impression it makes on us, and so, the anti-realist concludes, we should remain agnostic about the hidden forces and structures which scientists hypothesize about in their attempts to explain those impressions. There have also been theological arguments made on both sides of this debate. Some have argued that a good God would not seek to deceive us, and so the theories produced by our God-given powers of perception and reason

3. Francesco Stelluti's *Melissographia* (1625), produced using a microscope provided by Galileo, and dedicated to Pope Urban VIII.

should be trusted. Others suggest (like Urban VIII) that an all-powerful God need not have made creation fully comprehensible to finite beings. For them, anti-realism is a form of epistemological humility.

Modern debates about scientific realism have centred on the question of science's success. Realists argue that accurate predictions made by scientific theories that rely on entities that are unobservable—quantum physics, for instance—would be inexplicable unless those entities, such as electrons, actually existed and had the properties scientists ascribed to them. Anti-realists have a couple of good responses to this. First, they can point out that the history of science is a graveyard of now-abandoned theories which were once the most successful available but which posited entities we now do not believe existed. This would apply to the 16th-century theory that the planets were carried in their orbits by crystalline spheres; the 18th-century theory that explained combustion, according to which a substance known as 'phlogiston' was given off when things burned; or the 'ether' of 19th-century physics—a physical medium that was supposed to be necessary for the propagation of electromagnetic waves. Since theories we now take to be untrue have made successful predictions in the past (including also Ptolemaic astronomy, which was hugely successful for many centuries), there is no reason to suppose that today's successful theories are based on accurate descriptions of unobservable entities. Both true and untrue theories can produce accurate empirical predictions.

A second anti-realist argument was put forward by two influential philosophers of science in the 20th century—Thomas Kuhn and Bas van Fraassen. Kuhn's book, *The Structure of Scientific Revolutions* (1962), has become a classic in the field and remains one of the most widely read books about scientific knowledge. The book focused on what Kuhn called 'paradigm shifts' in the history of science, when one dominant world-view was replaced by another, as in the case of Copernican astronomy replacing the

Ptolemaic theory, or Einsteinian physics replacing pure Newtonianism. Kuhn did not think that newer paradigms replaced old ones because they were more accurate descriptions of reality, but rather that they had been chosen by the scientific community from among the various proposed theories because of their improved predictive power and puzzle-solving ability. Van Fraassen's 1980 book *The Scientific Image* made use of a 'Darwinian' explanation of the success of science. Since scientists will discard theories that make false predictions (as nature discards non-adaptive variations) and keep hold of those that make successful predictions, the fact that as time goes on their predictions get better is no surprise at all. They were selected for precisely their instrumental success, and there is no need for a further appeal to unobservable realities to explain that success.

Science and religion have a shared concern with the relationship between the observable and the unobservable. The Nicene Creed includes the statement that God made 'all that is, seen and unseen'. St Paul wrote in his letter to the Romans that 'since the creation of the world God's invisible qualities—his eternal power and divine nature—have been clearly seen, being understood from what has been made'. However, there are theological anti-realists too. The intuition here is similar to that of the scientific anti-realist. We have no way (at least not yet) to check our ideas about God against ultimate reality, and so propositions about God derived from scripture, tradition, or reason should not be treated as literally true but only as attempts by finite, fallible humans to make sense of those ideas. Theological anti-realism is sometimes misinterpreted as agnosticism or atheism, but the claim that God cannot fully be known is distinct from the claim that there is no God (or that we cannot know if there is). There is also a more orthodox tradition of mystical and 'negative' theology which emphasizes the gulf between the transcendence of God and the limited cognitive powers of mere humans, and draws the conclusion that it would be presumptuous to suppose any human formulation could grasp divine reality. Theologians in several religious traditions have responded to anti-realist calls for epistemic humility by claiming that the prospect of certainty, knowledge of real truth, is not a feat of human intellect, but requires divine intercession itself. For that reason, many have continued to try to look beyond the seen to the unseen, hoping to succeed in the apparently impossible task of drawing back the veil of phenomena to discover how things really are.

Galileo believed that what he saw through his telescope was real and that the Copernican model was not just instrumentally useful, but a true description of a universe governed by real unseen forces and laws. He explained the apparent contradiction of some biblical passages with this view of the solar system by treating scripture, in those cases, as instrumentally useful, rather than literally true. Among the many who, like Galileo, believe they have succeeded in seeing behind the veil of phenomena, there are conflicting accounts of what is to be found there—an impersonal cosmic machine, a chaos of matter in motion, a system governed by strict natural laws, or an omnipotent God acting in and through his creation. Which should we believe?

Chapter 3
God and nature

Even before there was science, people had intuitions about how the world around them typically behaved. Liquids flow downhill. Wounds take time to heal (and some are beyond complete healing). The realist might explain these ordinary phenomena as consequences of laws built in to the very structure of the universe itself, while an anti-realist might emphasize the way that repeated observations and shared experiences shape people's intuitions of what's ordinary. A religious philosopher might interpret the recurrence of everyday events as proof that God ordered the world in a purposeful, understandable way. But when something extraordinary happens, when something seemingly impossible or unexpected is observed, other explanations have to be considered.

Extraordinary events have historically performed an important social function. They have sometimes been interpreted as signs and wonders that mark out individuals, movements, or institutions as endowed with special God-given authority. The ability to perform miracles has been ascribed to revolutionaries, teachers, prophets, saints, and even to places and objects. The apparent power to resist the most irresistible of all forces—the laws of nature—has provided inspiration and hope to many communities facing persecution, poverty, or disaster.

4. St Agatha carrying her breasts on a plate, as depicted by the 17th-century painter Francisco de Zurbarán.

Take, for example, the story of Agatha, a 15-year-old girl in 3rd-century Sicily, then part of the Roman empire (Figure 4). She rejected the amorous advances of a local official, who banished her to a local brothel as revenge. When Agatha still refused to give up either her chastity or her Christian faith, she was tortured, including having her breasts cut off with pincers. A vision of St Peter appeared to her and healed her wounds. Agatha was then condemned to further abuses, including being dragged across burning coals and broken glass. During this ordeal, an earthquake was sent by God, killing several Roman officials. Agatha herself died in prison soon after.

The story of St Agatha did not end with her death. She was adopted by the people of Catania (in Sicily) as their protector and patron saint. According to local folklore, in the year after her martyrdom Mount Etna erupted. When her veil was held up towards the lava, it changed direction, leaving the city unharmed. Agatha's veil is reported to have protected the inhabitants of Catania from volcanic eruptions in the same miraculous way on several subsequent occasions. St Agatha's intercession is also credited by some believers with preventing the plague from spreading to Catania in 1743.

Natural and supernatural

Seeking miraculous intervention as protection against natural disasters shows one facet of the complex interaction between the natural and supernatural in religious thinking. For many who assert that God created the world, this includes the creation of natural principles that dictate, for instance, how volcanoes form or how lava flows. A volcano may be a part of nature, but for the believers of Agatha's day it was also created by God. God cared for the people of Catania and, because of St Agatha, would protect them, even if it meant momentarily suspending or contravening natural processes.

God's ability, either directly or through the intercession of saints and prophets, to contravene the laws of nature has long been central to many beliefs asserted by the Abrahamic religious traditions. God's various revelations to Moses, to St Paul and the apostles, and through the angel Gabriel to Muhammad are presented as miraculous. The Bible records that God sent plagues upon the Egyptians to punish them, divided the Red Sea, and provided manna from heaven to feed his chosen people. The Gospels assert that Jesus walked on water, healed the sick, brought the dead back to life, and was himself miraculously resurrected after dying on the cross. The Qur'ān includes reports of miracles performed by Moses and Jesus, including an episode, not included in the Christian Bible, when Jesus is said to have fashioned clay into the shape of a bird and miraculously breathed life into it to create a real bird. Although Muslims debate whether Muhammad himself performed miracles, there is a reference in the Qur'ān to the splitting of the Moon, which was interpreted as miraculous confirmation of Muhammad's prophetic status.

Reports of miracles persist to this day. They frequently come in the form of miraculous cures, such as those sought by pilgrims to the shrine of the Blessed Virgin Mary at Lourdes in France, or by those who attend revivalist religious meetings presided over by charismatic preachers offering divine healing. In 1995, milk sales across the world increased after reports that statues of the Hindu deities Ganesh and Shiva had seemed to drink spoonfuls of milk. In 2018, a Catholic church in New Mexico reported that its bronze statue of the Virgin Mary appeared to 'weep' olive oil.

In most cases, a rational and scientific explanation is soon forthcoming. In the case of the Hindu deities apparently drinking milk, it seemed the liquid was being drawn out of the spoon by capillary action (the same process that allows sponges and paper towels to absorb liquid), and was then simply running down the front of the statue. There was also a political explanation readily to hand. The ruling Congress Party in India claimed that news of the alleged miracle was being spread by their Hindu nationalist opponents for electoral gain. The leader of one right-wing Hindu party, speaking in defence of the miracle, said: 'Scientists who dismiss it are talking nonsense. Most of them are atheists and communists.'

Signs, wonders, and miracles have a central place in many religious traditions, whether as evidence of the special status of particular individuals, as proofs of particular doctrines, or as support for the broader social and political aspirations of a movement. Although some believers welcome miracles as apparent proofs of the reality and power of God, others are embarrassed by them. Reports of supernatural phenomena are all too often debunked, shown to be the results of wishful thinking, gullibility, or even fraud. Easily refuted claims of miracles can make religion seem superstitious and primitive.

But scepticism about miracles isn't the same as doubting religion entirely. Not every doctrine is rooted in either direct revelation from God or supernatural explanations of events. As mentioned previously, some religious groups envision God as author of a 'book of nature' as well as a (miraculously revealed) book of scripture. Justifications for arguments pertaining to God's existence, goodness, or power—or the moral rules people ought to live by—are often found in the natural world instead of (or in addition to) a sacred text. For many people, the distinction between science and religion is not the same as the difference between the natural and the supernatural; it is drawn instead between different explanations of both apparently natural and apparently non-natural phenomena.

The theologians' dilemma

Pity the poor theologians! They are faced with a seemingly impossible dilemma when it comes to making sense of divine action in the world. If they affirm that God does act through miraculous interventions in nature, then they must explain why God acts on some occasions but not on numerous others; why miracles are so poorly attested; and how they are supposed to be compatible with our scientific understanding of the universe. On the other hand, if they deny that God acts through special miraculous interventions, then they are left with questions about how much power God has to affect our lives and why one should bother with prayer or with following rules of ethical behaviour. The theologian seems to have to choose between a capricious, wonder-working, tinkering God and an absent, uninterested, undetectable one. Neither sounds like a suitable object for love and worship.

The theologian's task is to articulate how God can act in and through nature while avoiding the two unattractive caricatures indicated above. Various distinctions have been employed to try to achieve this. One of these differentiates between the basic primary cause of all reality, which is God, and the secondary, natural causes employed to achieve divine purposes. Another distinguishes between God's 'general providence'—the way that nature and history have been set up to unfold according to the divine will—and rare acts of 'special providence', or miracles, in which God's power is more directly manifest. If those acts of special providence are restricted to a very small number—perhaps only those attested in scripture, or those associated with the lives of a very small number of important prophetic individuals—then God's interventions in the world might seem less capricious. Among Christians, Muslims, and Jews there are those who believe that the age of God's revelations and miracles has now passed.

'As if God lived in the gaps?'

Protestant theologians have traditionally been somewhat more suspicious than Catholics about miracles (other than those explicitly recorded in the Bible). At the time of the Reformation, Protestants used the Catholic veneration of saints—especially the

Blessed Virgin Mary—and belief in the miraculous powers of holy relics, to portray the Church of Rome as superstitious and idolatrous. In more recent times, evangelical and Pentecostal forms of Protestant worship have involved wonders and miracles such as healings and speaking in tongues. However, there has been a continuous tradition of Protestant thought asserting that the age of miracles has passed and that divine activity is to be perceived in nature and history as a whole rather than in special interventions.

Two Protestant theologians illustrate this reinterpretation of the miraculous. The German thinker Friedrich Schleiermacher went so far as to redefine 'miracle' as 'merely the religious name for event', rather than as a happening which violated the laws of nature. In other words, a miracle was in the eye of the believer. In a series of lectures delivered in Boston in 1893, the Scottish evangelical theologian Henry Drummond, engaging the question of the proper Christian attitude to the theory of evolution, declared that a miracle was 'not something quick'. Rather, the whole, slow process of evolution was miraculous. Through that process God had produced not only the mountains and valleys, the sky and sea, the flowers and stars, but also 'that which of all other things in the universe commends itself, with increasing sureness as time goes on, to the reason and to the heart of Humanity—Love. Love is the final result of Evolution.' Drummond's conclusion was that it was this result—love—rather than the particular process, natural or supernatural, which was the real miracle.

In these same lectures Drummond introduced the idea of the 'God of the gaps'. He spoke of those 'reverent minds who ceaselessly scan the fields of Nature and the books of Science in search of gaps—gaps which they will fill up with God. As if God lived in the gaps?' God, he said, should be sought in human knowledge, not in human ignorance. He pointed out that if God is only to be found in special and occasional acts, then God must be supposed to be absent from the world the majority of the time. He asked whether the nobler conception was of a God present in everything or one present in occasional miracles. Drummond concluded that 'the idea of an immanent God, which is the God of Evolution, is infinitely grander than the occasional wonder-worker, who is the God of an old theology'.

The whole history of modern science could be read as a parable reinforcing Drummond's warning against placing God in the gaps of our current knowledge of nature. When Isaac Newton faced questions about why the planets remained in their orbits rather than gradually slowing down and falling towards the Sun and why distant stars were not drawn towards each other by gravity, he was prepared to hypothesize that God must intervene occasionally to keep the stars and planets in their proper positions. Newton's rival and critic G. W. Leibniz attacked this hypothesis on theological grounds. Newton's God, Leibniz wrote in 1715, lacking sufficient foresight to make a properly functioning universe at the first attempt, apparently needed 'to *wind up* his watch from time to time' and 'to *clean* it now and then' and 'even to *mend* it, as a clockmaker mends his work; who must consequently be so much the more unskilful a workman, as he is oftener obliged to mend his work and to set it right'. Leibniz preferred to see God's involvement in the universe as one of perfect and complete foresight. As theoretical and mathematical models of the solar system became even more accurate during the 18th and 19th centuries, there were those who went even further. When asked by Napoleon about the place of God in his cosmological system, the French physicist Pierre Simon de Laplace allegedly replied that he 'had no need for that hypothesis'.

The histories of geology, natural history, and biology reveal a similar pattern of supernatural explanations for things in the world (floods, volcanoes, and earthquakes; separate creations of different species; intelligent design of individual adaptations of creatures to their environments) gradually being pushed out in favour of more gradual, uniform, and lawlike natural processes. Even Charles Darwin's *The Origin of Species* made references to God, but only as the author of the laws of nature—those 'secondary causes' which seemed to be able to achieve the most wondrous results when impressed on matter, without apparent need for further interventions by the Creator.

The laws of nature

It was never the intention of the pioneers of modern science—people such as Isaac Newton, Robert Boyle, or René Descartes—to undermine religious belief. Far from it. They envisaged nature as an orderly system of mechanical interactions governed by mathematical laws and they hoped that people would see in this new vision the strongest possible evidence of divine power and intelligence. In 1630 Descartes wrote to the Catholic theologian Marin Mersenne: 'God sets up mathematical laws in nature as a king sets up laws in his kingdom.' Most early modern European scientists believed that God, who was responsible for determining the regular way in which nature would normally operate, was also capable of suspending or altering that normal course of nature at any time. Natural and supernatural explanations sometimes went hand in hand. Accepting supernatural events did not mean simply rejecting natural law. In fact, without a belief about the way nature 'normally' behaves, it would be impossible to recognize specific events as supernatural. Nonetheless, the method they adopted was one that favoured a view of God as lawgiver rather than as interventionist wonder-worker.

The collaborative enterprise inaugurated by these scientific pioneers has proceeded on the assumption that natural phenomena are indeed governed by strict laws. Does the success of science in explaining nature in terms of such laws amount to proof that God cannot act in nature, or is the coherent lawlike behaviour of the universe itself proof of God's creative power? One common explanation for the tendency of nature to follow laws (articulated in different degrees by various European early modern philosophers and theologians) is that God chooses to act within the bounds of natural laws, not because God is prevented from doing otherwise, but because God wants to be understood. As Descartes put it, God, being good, is not a 'deceiver' and would not trick people into believing in natural laws that were not real. Taking this further, English thinkers like Boyle and later William Paley both argued that God wanted people to observe divine presence through public evidence, whose experience we can share and discuss with others, not just through private miracles and revelations.

There are different ways of thinking about laws of nature. Realists and anti-realists have different opinions about whether such 'laws' have a real existence as entities or forces that constrain the world we observe. Natural laws can be interpreted in a more modest way as the best empirical generalizations we have so far arrived at to describe the behaviour of particular systems in particular contexts (often highly restricted experimental conditions that can be created only in laboratories). In addition, historians and other scholars of science and society debate whether laws of nature are solely rooted in the physical properties of the external world, or reflect the cultural norms of science in the times and places they were discovered and expressed.

Those who hold that the laws of nature are really built into the universe itself (regardless of whether or not they believe that this was done by a God creating the universe) sometimes insist that the patterns described as laws in various scientific fields ought to integrate with one another. This is sometimes called *reductionism*. For example, Descartes sought to discover and express laws of the physics of motion that were consistent with his theories of the human body and human psychology (and possibly also with his Catholic belief in free will). In the 20th century, some philosophers sought to 'unify' science by using logic to analyse statements used to describe observations and theories in different fields. These logical positivists hypothesized that statements in one science, say meteorology, could be 'reduced' or translated into statements that made sense within the language of another science, like physics. Critics of this reductionism argue that more complex systems, such as the biological processes of life, or psychological or sociological phenomena, cannot be explained in terms of the more 'fundamental' laws of physics that govern atoms and energy.

Reconciling natural laws at different levels has proven to be a complicated task for scientists and philosophers for the past century. Two of the most successful physical theories—general relativity and quantum mechanics—are both supposed to apply universally and yet are not compatible with each other. As the philosopher of science Nancy Cartwright has put it, what modern science seems to show is not that we live in a world governed by a single systematic set of natural laws that apply at all times and in all places, but rather that we live in a 'dappled world' in which pockets of order emerge, or can be made to emerge, using a patchwork of different scientific theories (from physics, to biology, to economics), none of which is applicable across all domains.

In contrast to reductionism, some philosophers of science speak of 'emergence', a phenomenon whereby properties that are not present at a more 'basic' physical level become apparent only in more complex systems. Ecosystems, which rely upon complex interactions among various species and their environment, follow certain laws which may not be observed when constituent species are considered separately under laboratory conditions. Even non-living systems, such as complex meteorological phenomena, cannot be explained or predicted purely through the laws governing the physics of gases and liquids. This idea of 'emergence' has also long been favoured by theologians seeking to reconcile religion and science as an argument against a deterministic universe in which everything in the universe unfolds according to natural laws without any ongoing creative input.

Emergence is also put forward as a potential explanation for spiritual realities that can be seen or felt socially or psychologically, but are not explained at the atomic level.

Quantum mechanics

In addition to the considerable philosophical perplexities involved in articulating, let alone defending, any kind of determinism, an important scientific challenge to the doctrine arose in the early 20th century in the form of quantum mechanics. Quantum theory resulted from physicists' attempts to understand the world of the very small—the behaviour of atomic and subatomic particles. Max Planck and Albert Einstein showed that light, then understood as an electromagnetic wave, also behaved as if it were made up of discrete particles, which came to be known as 'photons'. The implications of the theories later developed in the 1920s by quantum pioneers such as Erwin Schrödinger and Werner Heisenberg were wide-ranging, and their interpretation is still the subject of controversy. Einstein himself was unhappy with the probabilistic and indeterministic interpretations of quantum theory that came to predominate, saying that 'God does not play dice with the universe.' Some philosophers and physicists still share Einstein's unease. Having an instinctive preference for deterministic explanations, they hope to find a different interpretation of the laws of quantum physics.

Quantum theory is controversial because it seems to suggest that physics can no longer be reduced to a series of deterministic interactions between particles of matter. According to quantum theory, entities such as photons and electrons behave like either particles or waves depending on how the experimental apparatus interacts with them. Heisenberg's uncertainty principle further dictates that there is a limit to the precision with which the momentum and the position of a quantum entity can be known; exact knowledge of both at the same time is impossible. Finally, quantum phenomena can only be understood as functions of statistical probability. We might be able to predict that a certain percentage of radioactive atoms will decay over a specified period of time (this is where the concept of 'half-life' comes from and this process is crucial to studies concerning the age of the Earth and fossils found within it). However, quantum mechanics states that we cannot predict exactly when any given atom will decay.

Even this brief and inexpert summary of some of the findings of quantum physics is hopefully enough to give a sense of how far we have come from the world of classical materialistic determinism. Quantum mechanics suggests that at the most basic level material reality is not deterministic (nor does it always seem to be 'material'). We are in a world of clouds, of wave functions, of probabilities—not the reassuringly picturable clockwork universe of the Enlightenment. Quantum theory may even undermine the idea that the physical world exists objectively and independently of human observers, since the act of observation or measurement causes changes in physical objects.

Quantum physics is an absolutely central part of present-day science, and the fact that the picture of physical reality that it offers is so counter-intuitive and indeterministic has proved of great interest to philosophical and religious thinkers. The prospect of a new and more holistic philosophy of nature in which the observer is integrally involved and in which determinism is denied is one that appeals to proponents of many different world-views, from traditional religions to more modern 'New Age' ideologies. Attempts by theologians to make use of quantum physics as a more permanent source of 'gaps' in which God might be able to act have had a mixed reception. Such attempts do not help to answer the question of why God would act on some occasions rather than others; nor do they satisfy those religious believers who hold that, as the author rather than the slave of the laws of nature, God can override or suspend them at will without needing to tinker with the states of quantum systems. The fact that 'gaps' in natural explanation are frequently closed by new scientific

knowledge or the concern that a God-of-the-gaps seems limited
in power or scope are important criticisms of such arguments.
But for centuries, theologians and many religious scientists
professed a more general objection to such reasoning. For them
God was not found by the failure to explain things according to
nature, but by the very fact that nature worked and showed
evidence of a divine plan. This was a central idea within the
domain of natural theology.

Natural theology

Natural theology is the practice of trying to draw inferences about
God using our natural powers of sense and reason, rather than
relying on revelation or scripture. This has often included
arguments based on the natural world and its apparent design.
In the traditions of the major monotheistic religions, natural
theology was not developed to replace revealed scripture, but to
work in tandem with sacred texts to further knowledge about
divine intention, moral behaviour, and even the appropriate legal
and political systems used to govern nations. In a sense, natural
theology is the exact opposite of what Henry Drummond called
the 'God of the gaps'. Rather than finding evidence for God in
phenomena that cannot be explained by natural laws, natural
theology often draws argumentative force from the very fact that
the world does obey some sort of governing principles. The result
is not just an argument that science and religion might be
compatible, but a different view of what God might be and how
knowledge of a deity is found.

In the 13th century, Thomas Aquinas penned the *Summa
Theologiae*, perhaps the most influential work of Christian
theology of the entire millennium. In part of this magisterial
work, Aquinas put forward the 'quinque viæ'—the 'five ways' to
infer God's existence. Looking at phenomena such as the ability
of one natural cause to lead to a natural effect, which in turn
causes other natural effects, Aquinas reasons that there must

have been some initial first effect that had no natural cause. Another argument infers a designing mind from the observation that natural objects seem to act together in ways that accomplish unified purposes. Everything we observe exists temporarily and eventually decays or ends. Nothing on Earth has inevitable existence, but rather comes about as a contingent or accidental effect. Aquinas argues that such temporary things could not have come into being from nothing, thus there must be something in the world whose existence is necessary and permanent.

Though the five ways have sometimes been spoken of as 'proofs' of the existence of God, we should not imagine that these arguments were the only thing standing between Aquinas and atheism. The point of his 'five ways' was to examine both the justifications for faith that Christians already professed and to consider what else might be known about God besides sheer existence. The God Aquinas argued for has the ability to create and change things, is eternal, and has a purpose in mind for creation. From these attributes, Aquinas builds his system of theology.

Aquinas's theology has had a lasting impact on Christian thought, especially in shaping the way that the Catholic Church has responded to new scientific discoveries in the 20th and 21st centuries. In 1951, Pope Pius XII addressed the Pontifical Academy of Sciences discussing 'The Proof of God in the Light of Modern Natural Science'. The speech was widely misreported as a papal endorsement of the Big Bang theory (a cosmological account of the universe's beginning that at the time was not yet widely accepted). But Pius's real intention was to show that 20th-century discoveries about the changing nature of atoms, the impermanence of stars and galaxies, and even new understanding about heredity and evolution only demonstrated that Aquinas's arguments held up in the newly understood realms of the macrocosm and the infinitesimal.

The assertion that people could do theology—could determine truths about God and divine intentions—through examining nature, and more broadly by using their unaided powers of natural reason, had an especially complicated impact on Christian thought in the centuries after Aquinas, especially as European philosophy began to envision 'religion' and 'science' as distinct and independent forms of knowledge. Francis Bacon argued that 'the contemplations of man' could be divided into three categories, those which 'penetrate unto God', those 'circumferred to nature', and those 'reflected or reverted upon himself'. He placed natural theology in the first of these categories (distinct from inspired or revealed theology), describing it as 'that knowledge or rudiment of knowledge concerning God which may be obtained by the contemplation of His creatures'. Natural theology made use of natural knowledge, but not for the sole sake of understanding or explaining the natural world.

Natural theology and the idea that the natural world was a source of knowledge about God played an important role in 17th- and 18th-century England, when conflicts between members of the established Church of England, English Catholics, and dissenting English Protestants continually reshaped the relationship between the monarchy, parliament, and the people. The Royal Society of London, today the oldest continuous scientific society in existence, was established in 1660 upon the Restoration of the English monarchy. Explicitly established to be a religiously tolerant body, the Society prohibited discussion of religion or politics at its meetings. As the historians Steven Shapin and Simon Schaffer argue, its founder Robert Boyle believed that shared public experience and consensus could establish 'matters of fact', empirical knowledge distinct from its theological or metaphysical implications. Not that Boyle was unconcerned with natural theology. He posthumously endowed a series of lectures devoted to illustrating the harmonious relationship between Christianity and natural philosophy. The series was revived in 2004. The annual Boyle lecture has since been delivered at St Mary-le-Bow church in London.

In 1691, a year before the first Boyle Lecture, English naturalist John Ray published *The Wisdom of God Manifested in the Works of the Creation*. Ray was a member of the Royal Society and one of the first people to propose a formal classification system for plants and animals. His book drew on his unequalled knowledge of living creatures, showing how various species had bodies and behaviours that demonstrated their part in a divine plan. Ray argued that natural theology was not just about refuting atheism or logically inferring the powers and attributes of God. Deep understanding of the natural world and how creatures relate to one another and to their environment inspires a deep emotional response, producing feelings of awe and wonder wherein God is truly found. In one of the most striking passages, Ray argues that human beings were created with the ability to bend their necks to look straight up—which many other animals cannot do—precisely because the Creator wanted people to be able to gaze upon the heavens and be inspired by them.

This increased focus on natural theology as more than just a logical proof of God's existence illustrates how the genre of natural theology evolved over the 18th and 19th centuries. Building upon works like Ray's, a number of lectures and publications in English began to view the goal of natural theology as something more than drawing inferences about God from the evidence of nature. They invoked the idea that God was all knowing or good, or had human well-being in mind as a way to explain how nature itself worked. By the middle of the 19th century, natural theology and the kind of thinking it entailed had a strong influence on a new genre of publishing that came to be known as 'popular science'. The *Bridgewater Treatises*, a series of eight books on natural theology, were published in the 1830s. Though the theological arguments presented in the treatises were often unoriginal, the great appeal of these best-selling books lay in the rigour of their descriptions of the natural world. In practice, historian Jonathan Topham argues, their success was rooted in giving a religiously respectable cover to studying the natural world. 'They presented the pious middle classes with a largely nontechnical and religiously conservative compendium of contemporary science.'

Hume, Paley, and the politics of natural religion

Natural theology, both as a form of popular science communication and as a way of thinking about religion, flourished greatly in England and Scotland in the 17th and 18th centuries— more so than in most other Christian countries of Europe. Some historians have attributed this to a tradition of British empiricism that developed in contrast to 'continental' rationalism. But also important is the place of religion in Britain. Although many religious Protestants who dissented from the established Church of England gained the right to profess their faith with the Toleration Act of 1689, Catholics and Unitarians (as well as non-Christians) were excluded from this toleration. Throughout the 1700s anyone wishing to attend Oxford or Cambridge universities, or to hold public office, was required to swear their subscription to the Church of England's Articles of Faith.

In this political context, the critiques of natural and revealed religion developed by the Scottish philosopher David Hume (1711–76) were in no small part a rejection of the use of state power to compel belief.

Hume was the author of some of the most famous expressions of rationalist scepticism about religion—taking aim at both supernatural and natural theological ideas. In a 1748 essay 'Of Miracles', for instance, Hume argued against miracles on the basis of the relative weakness of the evidence in favour of them. Since the laws of nature are, by definition, generalizations that conform as closely as possible to the universal experience of humanity, Hume said, then they are as empirically well grounded as any statement can be. However generous we wish to be about the strength of the evidence in favour of miracles—that is, the reports of supposed eye-witnesses to the events, such as those recorded in the scriptures and in lives of saints—that testimony will never be as strong as the evidence that supports the laws of nature. Which, Hume asked, would be the greater miracle—that the laws of nature had actually been overturned or that those attesting to the miracle (possibly even including yourself) were mistaken? A rational person, Hume concluded, would have to answer that the falsity of the testimony was the more likely option. In short, a rational person could not believe in miracles. To put this in terms of the different sources of knowledge discussed in Chapter 2, Hume's argument was that collective sense experience trumps testimony.

In earlier writings, Hume had introduced what philosophers of science often call the 'problem of induction'. The practice of drawing general conclusions from patterns of separate observable facts—the process of induction—cannot be philosophically validated except through circular reasoning. That is, the justification for why induction seems to work is through an inductive process of observing its utility in previous cases. Although it might at first seem that natural theology, in the form modelled by Royal Society members like Boyle and Ray, might be the kind of collective sense experience that Hume would prefer to testimony or revealed religion, Hume extended his philosophical scepticism to religious arguments inferred from nature in his posthumous *Dialogue Concerning Natural Religion* (1779).

Much like Galileo's *Dialogue Concerning the Two Chief World Systems* (which Hume refers to), the *Dialogue* is written in the form of a three-way discussion among people representing different philosophical positions. The scientific sceptic Philo demolishes the arguments of both Demea (who argues dogmatically for a God based upon a priori rational argument and revelation) and Cleanthes, who serves as the mouthpiece for natural theology. Philo tells Cleanthes that reasoning that nature looks as though it is designed because it resembles human inventions is flawed. To claim to know what God's purposes are is to imagine a God who is limited and anthropomorphic, not infinite and all powerful. Moreover, Philo claims, knowing only this one particular world created by God (or perhaps even by a number of deities working at cross purposes) we cannot even infer that this world is good. 'In a word, Cleanthes, a man, who follows your hypothesis, is able, perhaps, to assert, or conjecture, that the universe, sometime, arose from something like design: But beyond that position he cannot ascertain one single circumstance, and is left afterwards to fix every point of his theology, by the utmost licence of fancy and hypothesis.'

Hume's arguments against natural theology have long been viewed as formidable by philosophers of science. It is not uncommon to see philosophers claim that Hume refuted the arguments of William Paley (1743–1805) despite the fact that Paley's *Natural Theology* was published a quarter-century after Hume died. Paley's work is in part a response to Hume, as well as a commentary on the religious politics of his time. An Anglican clergyman, philosopher, and theologian, Paley was one of the most popular English religious writers of the 18th and 19th centuries. His *Principles of Moral and Political Philosophy* (1785) became a standard text at Cambridge and many American universities. Although part of the Church of England, Paley was also outspoken against the requirement of demanding oaths of adherence to the established church as a prerequisite for positions of authority and power. This was not because he thought that other religious interpretations might also be correct, but because he thought that providing incentives for dissenters to swear oaths they did not believe in put their souls in greater peril than simply holding to unorthodox ideas. In part, he wrote his major works as a means to persuade his audience of Anglican interpretations of God's place in nature without using the brute force of economic and social pressure.

Paley argued for a kind of utilitarianism, arguing that the world that God created was so constructed as to bring about the greatest possible amount of well-being and happiness. This did not mean a world without suffering—Paley observed that creatures must sometimes die for others to live—but he argued that in human affairs, a principle of optimizing well-being was both possible and desirable. Paley's politics were conservative and wary of social change; he argued that people were endowed with God-given instincts that suited them towards different occupations. When people went against divine inclinations—when the manual labourer wanted to act as the ruler—a well-ordered society breaks down. Paley attributed much of the suffering in France that followed its Revolution to this kind of failure. Paley's social theories were in dialogue with those of another Anglican clergyman, Thomas Malthus.

Malthus's concern was with human populations. He believed that these had a natural tendency to increase at a geometric rate from one generation to the next (1, 2, 4, 8 . . .), while the amount of food that a society could produce increased only arithmetically (1, 2, 3, 4 . . .). This led, in each generation, to a struggle for resources. The strong would survive but the weak would perish. Malthus's *Essay on the Principle of Population* (1798) argued that human suffering, such as war and famine, was unavoidable because human populations naturally grow faster than the resources needed to support them. This opposed Paley's idea that God had ensured that such widespread suffering could be avoided by rulers and societies that adhered to a divinely ordained moral order. Malthus interpreted this inevitable suffering theologically, arguing that God designed nature this way to spur humanity's intellectual and spiritual progress. 'Had population and food increased in the same ratio, it is probable that man might never have emerged from the savage state.'

Paley's *Natural Theology* attempted to show that his moral utilitarianism was illustrated in the natural world, demonstrating the goodness and personal interest of God in creation. At the same time, indebted to Hume, Paley's arguments were constructed more narrowly than precursors like John Ray. For Paley, the primary argument for God lay in evidence that the created world demonstrated purpose. For Paley, it did not logically matter how some object came to be created or even if it had existed perpetually in a universe of infinite duration. He deliberately set aside arguments about origins. Also sensitive to Hume's criticism that ascribing human-centred purposes to the natural world produced an anthropomorphic image of God, Paley even conceded that in some cases, the purpose of some feature of the natural world may not be known. However, Paley argued that the existence of purpose, what were often called 'final causes', could still be inferred by the fact that material objects in nature showed some kind of adaptation to the laws of nature. Thus, even if we did not know that vision was a form of sensation that creatures use to observe the world around them, the fact that the parts of the eye seem to demonstrate great attunement to the laws of optics is evidence that whatever caused eyes to exist had some purpose in mind that made use of the way light would pass through them.

Later defenders of natural theology, including many of the authors of the wide-selling *Bridgewater Treatises*, explicitly acknowledge Paley's work as definitive, even though the examples he cited from the natural world were sometimes seen as outdated by discoveries made in the 19th century. But some of these writers defended Paley's conclusions, that there was a single, beneficent, omnipresent God, by reverting to older natural theological arguments less carefully responsive to Hume. By the 1820s and 1830s, when Charles Darwin was a student, British natural theology had restored its focus on questions about how things in the world came to be created.

The political and ideological debates of this era were not seen as a conflict of science against religion, but instead were disagreements between different religious interpretations of how much nature and natural laws should shape understanding about God, in conjunction with questions about divine action, miracles, and revelation. Such questions are among the most difficult with which religious believers have to grapple. As Henry Drummond put it, 'If God appears periodically, He disappears periodically. If He comes upon the scene at special crises, He is absent from the scene in the intervals.' Science and philosophy certainly do not require us to believe in determinism or to deny the possibility of miracles. However, the theologians' dilemma will not go away: divine action and divine inaction are both hard to explain. And believers continue to disagree about whether God acts through the creation of natural laws, the violation of natural laws, or both.

Chapter 4
Darwin and evolution

When he died at his Kent home in April 1882, the English naturalist Charles Darwin was a worldwide celebrity, famed as the author of the theory of evolution that had transformed science and become the defining philosophy of the age. Despite lingering doubts about Darwin's religious beliefs, it was soon agreed that no other tribute would be adequate than a grand funeral at Westminster Abbey. The great and the good gathered to mark the astonishing theoretical achievements, the decades of patient research, and the dignity and modesty of this unassuming English gentleman. At the funeral, the Reverend Frederic Farrar's sermon compared Darwin's genius with that of his countryman Isaac Newton, next to whose memorial in the abbey Darwin's final resting place would be. Farrar explained that Darwin's theory was quite consistent with an elevated sense of the actions of the Creator in the natural world. The funeral symbolized the Anglican establishment's acceptance of Darwin and biological evolution, just over 20 years after the publication of *The Origin of Species* in 1859.

It was a somewhat suspicious and hesitant kind of acceptance, though. Not everyone in the Church of England, nor society at large, was happy to 'go the whole orang'—as geologist Charles Lyell described the belief that evolution applied to humans too. Indeed, it has always been *human* evolution in particular, rather than the evolution of bacteria, beetles, barnacles, or bats, that has really captured the imagination and unsettled the beliefs of the wider public. Religious ideas about the elevated place of humanity in creation, and especially about the soul and morality, were the ones most directly challenged by the evolutionary science that Darwin's career helped to establish as a new orthodoxy. The idea of evolution's conflict with a 'literal interpretation' of scripture was initially a fringe movement, gaining more traction only in the second half of the 20th century. For many others who have resisted Darwinism for religious reasons, their concern has been rooted in the theory of evolution's apparent incompatibility with free will, moral responsibility, and a rational and immortal human soul.

In this chapter, we explore these and other reasons why the theory of evolution has been considered so dangerous, starting with Darwin's religious views and the reception of his theory around the globe, before looking specifically at controversies about teaching evolution in schools. The personage of Charles Darwin himself continues to haunt these discussions. The theory of evolution by natural selection has become identified with this single iconic historical individual. The most frequently used pictures of Darwin are those from his old age in which his white beard and portentous expression conjure up images of biblical prophets, perhaps even of God. Darwin's personal scientific and religious beliefs are often discussed and sometimes cited as evidence of the real relationship between evolution and religion. It is important therefore to have a grasp of what this revolutionary scientific thinker really thought and why.

Darwin's odyssey

In his early 20s, Darwin was planning a career in the Church of England. He had embarked on medical training in Edinburgh a few years earlier but had found lectures boring and demonstrations of surgery disgusting. His father sent him off to

Christ's College, Cambridge, where young Charles signed up to the Thirty-Nine Articles of the Church of England and set about studying mathematics and theology with a view to entering holy orders. But Darwin found that theology appealed about as much as surgery. His real passion was for beetle-hunting rather than Bible-reading, and he had an early triumph when one of the specimens he had identified appeared in print in an instalment of *Illustrations of British Entomology*. In 1831 this enthusiastic young amateur naturalist was invited to join the HMS *Beagle* as a companion to the ship's captain, Robert Fitzroy, and to undertake collections and observations on matters of natural-historical interest. Perhaps he was not, after all, destined to become the Reverend Charles Darwin.

The primary purpose of the *Beagle*'s expedition was to complete the British Admiralty's survey of the coast of South America, but its five-year itinerary also took in Australia, New Zealand, and South Africa. Such expeditions were acts of hegemony and dominion over a vast proportion of the world's land, sea, and people. As Britain expanded its empire throughout the 19th century, collecting and interpreting the world's natural diversity, including geology, biology, and anthropology, became both a symbolic and very real tool of colonial power.

Darwin's observations of rock formations, plants, animals, and indigenous peoples were also central to his own intellectual development. Aboard the *Beagle*, Darwin's religious views started to evolve too. He had no doubt that the natural world was the work of God. In his notebook he recorded his impressions of the South American jungle: 'Twiners entwining twiners—tresses like hair—beautiful lepidoptera—Silence—hosannah.' To Darwin, these jungles were 'temples filled with the varied productions of the God of Nature', in which no one could stand without 'feeling that there is more in man than the mere breath of his body'. He even admired the role of Christian missionaries as colonizers, observing that 'so excellent is the Christian faith, that the outward conduct of the [indigenous] believers is said most decidedly to have been improved by its doctrines'.

After the voyage, however, Darwin would start to have doubts. His grandfather, father, and elder brother had all rejected Christianity, adopting either Deism or outright unbelief. He seemed to be heading in a similar direction. His reasons were many. His travels had revealed to him at first hand the great variety of religious beliefs and practices around the world. All these different religions claimed to have a special revelation from God, but they could not all be right. Then there was his moral revulsion at the Christian doctrine that while the faithful would be saved, unbelievers and heathens, along with unrepentant sinners, would be consigned to an eternity of damnation. Darwin thought this was a 'damnable doctrine' and could not see how anyone could wish it to be true. This objection hit him with particular force after the death of his unbelieving father in 1848. The death of his beloved young daughter Annie in 1851 prompted further painful thoughts about the question of an afterlife, along with grave reflections upon the cruelty of the natural world.

At the time he wrote *The Origin of Species* Darwin was still a theist, although not a Christian. By the end of his life he preferred to adopt the label 'agnostic', which had been coined by his friend Thomas Huxley in 1869. Darwin, for the most part, kept his religious doubts to himself. He had many reasons to do so, not least his desire for a quiet life and social respectability. The most important reason, though, was his wife Emma. In the early years of their marriage, Emma, a pious evangelical Christian, wrote a letter to Charles of her fears about his loss of faith in Christianity and the consequences for his salvation. She could not bear the thought that his doubts would mean they were not reunited after death in heaven.

Darwin's religious views changed during the same decades that he was developing his theory of evolution by natural selection, but it would be too simplistic to suggest that evolution made him a non-believer. His personal tragedies, experiments, journeys, and observations, his social position, and his education all informed the scientific and religious world-view he came to. What is true is that Darwin's understanding of the political, theological, and scientific thought of his time shaped his understanding of a new theory of biological change.

The theory of evolution by natural selection

When Darwin got back to England he began to focus on the 'species question'. This was the 'mystery of mysteries' for those seeking a naturalistic explanation of the origins of the different forms of life. In the 1830s, Darwin was confronted with two alternative explanations which were both equally unpalatable to him. Either each species had been created at a particular time and place by God, or else all life had started, perhaps spontaneously, in a simple form and had gradually climbed the ladder of life in the direction of greater complexity and perfection. The first option was unattractive because it posited a whole series of miraculous interventions in the history of life. What Darwin wanted to find was an explanation in terms of natural laws. The second option, the French naturalist Jean-Baptiste Lamarck's theory of 'transmutation', developed in his *Philosophie zoologique* (1809), involved too many unacceptable theoretical assumptions for Darwin, such as the idea that life was continuously being spontaneously generated and starting its ascent up the ladder of life, that all life was climbing in the same direction up this single ladder, and that a creature's own voluntary efforts could alter its physical structure. Lamarck's theory was also widely believed to be connected to religiously unacceptable ideas of materialism and determinism—in other words, to the view that all phenomena, both mental and physical, could ultimately be explained in terms of causal interactions between particles of matter. Radicals in England, some inspired by revolutionary events in France, also took Lamarckism as evidence against a hereditary upper class, arguing that differences in aptitude and intelligence were shaped by the environment and could improve or degenerate from one generation to the next.

A key component of Darwin's world-view was provided by a book he read during the *Beagle* voyage, Sir Charles Lyell's *Principles of Geology*, published in three volumes between 1830 and 1833. Lyell's book argued that the history of the Earth was one of gradual changes operating over long periods of time rather than one of regular violent catastrophes. This argument also implied that geological events like earthquakes and volcanic eruptions had natural causes, as sudden culminations after aeons of slow change. If geology could be explained by such gradual modifications over time, perhaps biology could too. Darwin later confessed, 'I always feel as if my books came half out of Lyell's brains.'

The animal life of the Galapagos islands—its finches and giant tortoises, its iguanas and mocking birds—was later to provide one of the keys to unlocking the 'mystery of mysteries'. Each island had its own species of finch, with differences in the sizes and shapes of their beaks (Figure 5). Did this require Darwin to believe that there had been a separate act of creation by God on each island, and another one on the mainland too? This seemed scientifically and theologically inelegant, to say the least. A unidirectional transmutationist model would not work either, since there was no obvious way to arrange these different species in a single line with one developing into the other. From the late 1830s, Darwin filled notebooks with arguments and counter-arguments trying to solve these sorts of problems. He thought about the way that breeders of pigeons selected particular individuals among each generation when trying to produce unusual new varieties. The analogy with artificial selection would be central to his argument. Even more central, though, was the idea of scarcity and competition for resources, which he borrowed from Malthus's *Essay on the Principle of Population*.

1. Geospiza magnirostris. 2. Geospiza fortis.
3. Geospiza parvula. 4. Certhidea olivasea.

5. An illustration from Darwin's *Journal of Researches into the Natural History and Geology of the Countries Visited During the Voyage of H.M.S. Beagle* (1845), showing a selection of the different species of finch collected during the voyage.

Darwin read Malthus's *Essay* in 1838 and saw how it could be applied to the species question. Looking at the entangled creepers of the South American jungle, the parasitic and murderous instincts of insects, and even at the plants and weeds in his own back garden, Darwin could see something similar going on—a competition for resources which those creatures with even a slight advantage over their competitors would win. This struggle for existence and the resulting 'survival of the fittest', as the evolutionary philosopher Herbert Spencer would call it, became the central idea of Darwin's theory. Alfred Russel Wallace, who came up with the idea of natural selection in the 1850s (20 years later than Darwin but before Darwin had published his theory), also credited Malthus as a source of inspiration.

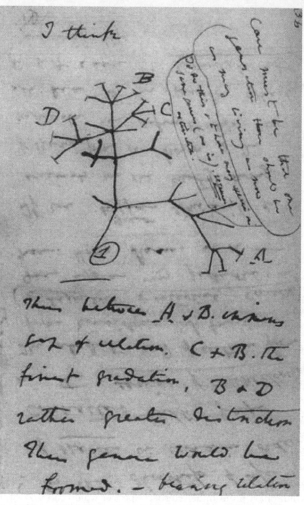

6. One of Darwin's first sketches, in his notebooks of the late 1830s, of his idea of a branching tree of life connecting all organisms through a shared ancestry.

Darwin now had his solution. The adaptation of organisms to their environment, and the origins of separate species, should be explained not in terms of direct divine acts of creation, but by geographical distribution, random heritable variation, competition for resources, and the survival of the fittest over vast spans of time. Natural selection could come in many different guises—as a disease, a predator, a drought, a shortage of your favourite food, a sudden change in the weather—but those individuals in each generation who happened by good luck to be the best equipped to cope with these natural assaults would flourish and leave offspring, while the less well adapted would perish without issue. Repeat that process for hundreds of millions of years and the whole panoply of species now observed could evolve from the simplest forms of life (Figure 6).

In 1858, Darwin received a letter from Wallace written from Ternate, part of the Dutch East Indies colony. The letter outlined a theory virtually identical to Darwin's and spurred him into a more rapid publication of his ideas than he had planned. At a hurriedly arranged meeting of the Linnaean Society, an announcement was made of Darwin's and Wallace's theories. The following year saw the publication by John Murray of Albemarle Street, London, of *The Origin of Species by Means of Natural Selection, or The Preservation of Favoured Races in the Struggle for Life*.

'Our unsuspected cousinship with the mushrooms'

On opening the *Origin* in 1859, the first words a reader would have come across were two theological epigraphs—one a quotation from William Whewell's Bridgewater Treatise, the other from Francis Bacon, one of the leading lights of the scientific revolution of the 17th century. Whewell stated that in the material world 'events are brought about not by insulated interpositions of Divine power, exerted in each particular case, but by the establishment of general laws'. According to Bacon, one could never have too much knowledge of either the book of God's word or the book of God's works, divinity or philosophy, 'rather let men endeavour an endless progress or proficience in both'.

Those first readers of *The Origin of Species* were presented with a view of nature in which God had been pushed to the margins but not banished completely. God was no longer needed to create each individual species but Darwin, whether for the sake of convention or out of his own remaining religious convictions, presented his argument as favouring a kind of theistic evolution. When it came to the concluding section of the book, Darwin reiterated Whewell's view that God acted in a lawlike rather than a miraculous fashion. 'To my mind,' Darwin wrote,

> it accords better with what we know of the laws impressed on matter by the Creator, that the production and extinction of the past and present inhabitants of the world should have been due to secondary causes ... When I view all beings not as special creations, but as the lineal descendants of some few beings which lived long before the first bed of the Silurian system was deposited, they seem to me to become ennobled.

In the famous closing sentences of the book, Darwin marvelled that from 'the war of nature, from famine and death', the highest forms of life had been produced. He concluded:

> There is grandeur in this view of life, with its several powers, having been originally breathed into a few forms or into one; and that, whilst this planet has gone cycling on according to the fixed law of gravity, from so simple a beginning endless forms most beautiful and most wonderful have been, and are being, evolved.

From the second edition onwards, in case there was any doubt about his meaning, he changed the phrase 'breathed into a few forms or into one' to 'breathed by the Creator into a few forms or into one'.

Darwin's rereading of the book of nature also gave him reasons to rethink his religion. Some theologians argued that the 'perfection' of organs was proof of their direct and divine creation. Hard though it was for him to believe it himself—the human eye could still give him a shudder of incredulity—he came to think that all these adaptations came about by natural processes. Variation and natural selection could, over time, produce 'organs of extreme perfection'. Even after abandoning the idea of distinct and supernatural acts of creation, Darwin still respected more subtle arguments like Paley's about nature's benevolent purpose, even citing Paley in the *Origin* to counter 'difficulties of the theory'. But eventually the suffering he'd seen both in his own life and in the natural world led him to conclude that Paley's argument 'which formerly seemed to me so conclusive, fails, now that the law of natural selection has been discovered'.

Darwin had observed all sorts of cruelty and violence in nature, which he could not believe a benevolent and omnipotent God could have willed. Why, for example, would God have created the ichneumon wasp? The ichneumon lays its eggs inside a caterpillar, with the effect that when the larvae hatch they eat their host alive. Why would God create cuckoos which eject their foster siblings from the nest? Why make ants that enslave other species of ant? Why give queen bees the instinct of murderous hatred towards their daughters? 'What a book a Devil's chaplain might write', Darwin exclaimed, 'on the clumsy, wasteful, blundering low & horridly cruel works of nature!'

There were some within the Christian churches who embraced Darwin's variety of natural theology. There was indeed greater grandeur and nobility, they agreed, as well as more simplicity and order, in a world where God had created through a lawlike process of evolution, rather than one in which God periodically intervened to top up the planet's flora and fauna after particularly destructive catastrophes.

Henry Drummond was one such individual. The historian, Christian socialist, and novelist Charles Kingsley was another. His famous children's story *The Water Babies*, published in 1863, included an allusion to his approval for Darwin's new theory. The little boy Tom approaches 'Mother Carey', a personification of nature, and says, 'I heard, ma'am, that you were always making new beasts out of old.' Mother Carey replies, 'So people fancy. But I am not going to trouble myself to make things, my little dear. I sit here and make them make themselves.' A future Archbishop of Canterbury, Frederick Temple, was another Anglican who supported the idea that God might have created through variation and natural selection rather than by a succession of miracles. On the other side of the Atlantic also there were individuals, such as the Harvard botanist and Presbyterian Asa Gray, who adopted theistic interpretations of Darwinian evolution.

But there were instances of conflict too, most famously in a dramatic confrontation at the British Association for the Advancement of Science in Oxford in 1860. Darwin himself was not present, but his theory was discussed in a paper applying Darwinian ideas to the question of intellectual and social progress. The general issue of Darwinism was then opened up to the floor for further debate. First, the Bishop of Oxford, Samuel Wilberforce, spoke at length about Darwin's theory. We do not have a record of exactly what he said, but we can infer from his review of the *Origin* published in the conservative *Quarterly Review*. Wilberforce conceded that the book's conclusion that 'mosses, grasses, turnips, oaks, worms, and flies, mites and elephants, infusoria and whales, tadpoles of today and venerable saurians, truffles and men, are all equally the lineal descendants of the same aboriginal common ancestor' was certainly surprising, but one which he would have to admit if the scientific reasoning were sound. He could not object to Darwin's inference of 'our unsuspected cousinship with the mushrooms' on biblical grounds, since it was most unwise to try to judge the truth of scientific theories with reference to revelation. However, drawing heavily on the work of the country's leading anatomist, Richard Owen, Wilberforce raised plenty of scientific objections to the theory, focusing especially on the lack of fossil evidence of transitional forms, and on the fact that, however many varieties of pigeons and dogs may have been produced under domestication, pigeons had always remained pigeons and dogs always dogs. There had been no hint of a new species.

Although he did not base his objections on a literal reading of the Bible, Wilberforce's resistance to evolution, like that of many religious believers since his day, did derive from a commitment to a biblically inspired world-view in which human beings were separate from and superior to the rest of the animal world. The Christian teaching that God took on human form in the person of Jesus Christ also gave that human form a unique significance. To claim that man was nothing more than an 'improved ape' rather than 'Creation's crown and perfection' was, Wilberforce pointed out, demeaning to God as well as to humanity. At the end of his remarks at Oxford, Wilberforce is reported to have turned to one of Darwin's staunchest advocates, Thomas Huxley, and asked whether he was descended from an ape on the side of his grandmother or his grandfather. It was intended as a joke, but Huxley was apparently white with anger as he rose and replied severely that he would rather be descended from an ape than from a man who used his intellect and influence to introduce ridicule into a grave scientific discussion. As the temperature in the packed auditorium rose, Darwin's old companion from HMS *Beagle*, Captain Fitzroy, stood up holding a Bible aloft with both hands and denounced Darwin's theory. Another of Darwin's inner circle, the botanist Joseph Hooker, then weighed in with what was, on Hooker's own account, a decisive intervention on the side of Darwinism.

It is a colourful story, and one that has become part of Darwinian folklore. In 1860, Wilberforce, Huxley, and Hooker all thought that they had won the day. But by the time the tale came into wider circulation a couple of decades later, Huxley and Hooker, who had long been pressing for the autonomy of science from the church, had risen to positions of greater influence. The ascendancy of the professionalizing agnostics within the British scientific establishment was witnessed by the fact that both Hooker and Huxley were chosen to serve as presidents of the Royal Society. The Huxley–Wilberforce story was then used retrospectively, as a piece of victors' history, to suggest a clearer triumph for scientific naturalism over Anglican conservatism than had really been achieved in Oxford in 1860. It suited the new elite to be able to tell the story in a way that seemed to foreshadow and legitimize their own rise to power, while simultaneously depoliticizing the issue. The 1860 confrontation between Samuel Wilberforce and Richard Owen, on the one hand, and the young Darwinians, on the other, had resulted from a struggle for dominance within the institutions of British science and education—a conflict between competing social interests as well as between competing interpretations of the scientific evidence for evolution. The later recasting of the Huxley–Wilberforce debate as one more instance of a simple and timeless conflict between 'science' and 'religion' helped to suggest that the agnostics' rise to power was the result of an inexorable historical process rather than a deliberate political campaign.

Evolution and theology

Wilberforce's review of *The Origin of Species* identified the theological issues which would play out repeatedly among Christians, Jews, Muslims, and others as they considered the implications of evolution for their religious beliefs in the 19th century and afterwards. Some of these were not new. Discoveries in astronomy and geology had already given theologians plenty of opportunity to discuss the relative authority of science and scripture in determining natural knowledge. Darwin's view of nature drew particular attention to suffering, violence, and death. But people hardly needed Darwin to tell them that these were features of the natural world in general and of human life in particular. Again, theologians were already aware of the problem of evil, and had various responses to it. One common response to human evil was to explain that God must allow his creatures free will, which could be turned to either good or evil ends. Bishop Wilberforce's response to Darwin's remarks on imperfections in nature, and on the apparent cruelty of such creatures as the ichneumon wasp, was to refer to the Christian idea of the Fall. On this view, when Adam and Eve, the crowns and rulers of creation, were expelled from the Garden of Eden for their disobedience, it was not just they and their human descendants who fell from grace into a disordered state; it was the whole of nature. As Wilberforce put it, the 'strange forms of imperfection and suffering amongst the works of God' were the ongoing expression of 'the strong shudder which ran through all this world when its head and ruler fell'.

What was theologically new and troubling was the destruction of the boundary securely separating humanity from the 'brute creation' (and, to a lesser but significant extent, the destruction of the boundaries separating kinds of plants and animals from each other). The publication of Darwin's theories about human evolution in *The Descent of Man* (1871) and *The Expression of the Emotions in Man and Animals* (1872) provided further material for discussions about the relationship between humanity and the other animals. In these works Darwin speculated, as he had not dared to in 1859, on how even the most elevated of human faculties—the emotions, the moral sense, and religious feelings—might have evolved by natural means.

By the end of the 19th century, there was no serious scientific opposition to the basic evolutionary tenets of descent with modification and the common ancestry of all forms of life. There was considerable dispute about the explanatory sufficiency of the mechanism identified by Darwin and Wallace as the main driving force of evolution, namely natural selection acting on random variations. Lamarckian mechanisms of the inheritance of acquired characteristics were still discussed, and the process of heredity was a matter of dispute. From 1900 onwards, there were debates about whether Gregor Mendel's work on all-or-nothing units of inheritance that came to be known as 'genes' was compatible with a Darwinian model of gradual change over generations. That debate was not resolved until the 1930s and 1940s with the modern evolutionary synthesis of neo-Darwinism. That framework combined Mendelian genetics and the theory of natural selection, and led to the rejection of evolutionary theories that appealed either to the inheritance of acquired characteristics or to some innate life-force driving evolution from within.

Throughout these decades, theologians continued to make various uses of evolutionary ideas. The early 20th century saw a flourishing of ideas about creative evolution and guided evolution that appealed to religious thinkers. Since then, the triumph of neo-Darwinism has posed different theological questions. Within each faith tradition, there have been those who embrace evolution but also those who question or reject it.

Evolution, religion, and empire

Darwin's journey on the *Beagle* was both enabled by and representative of the global power of the British empire. Throughout the 19th century, and well into the 20th, Britain and other national powers exercised various forms of colonial control over much of the world, including many parts of Africa and Asia—and used economic and military clout to influence cultural and political affairs elsewhere. While science and religion were sometimes thought to be in conflict by warring elite factions within these nations, they often worked together in promoting this kind of colonial domination. We have spoken already of Darwin's admiration for Christian missionaries, who, in his view improved the lot of more 'primitive' peoples by bringing them European religion. Darwin saw this first hand, when the *Beagle's*

Captain Fitzroy abducted several children in Tierra del Fuego and brought them to England to be 'civilized'. As missionaries, explorers, military leaders, and imperial officials sought to assert knowledge of and control over local populations, they also used their scientific systems of analysis and classification to justify their claims. The separation of knowledge into distinct categories of 'science' and 'religion', although still relatively new to Europe, was used by Europeans as a mark of civilization and sophistication that could justify their moral authority to govern people from other parts of the world and to lay claims to their lands, bodies, and resources. That other peoples had not segregated their knowledge in this way was seen (by Western colonizers) as proof of their inferiority.

Malthus's view that scarcity, competition, and limited survival had spurred the progress of civilization towards deeper theological and philosophical truths, and the natural theological idea that the created world had an ultimate purpose shaped by God's goodness, had been incorporated into Darwinian theories of species change to give rise to what is sometimes called 'Social Darwinism'. These ideas travelled with European and North American colonizers and were used to interpret the people they encountered. In framing a narrative of evolutionary progress, colonizers placed their own physical characteristics as most fully evolved away from other animal species and interpreted others as closer to animal relatives. The same was true of non-Western religions and cultures. Reports that indigenous people were animists (believers that physical objects were infused with spirits) or were polytheistic—or that they had not conceived of a distinction between rare miracles and natural law—were used to justify claims that they had not evolved as much as Europeans.

In using themselves as the standards by which the assessment of other peoples was calibrated, colonizers placed their own invention—the knowledge tradition they called 'science'—as the most highly evolved form of thought. Other forms of natural knowledge, if they could not be explained in a scientific way, were often dismissed. In realist terms, it did not matter whether indigenous forms of knowledge—about navigation, medicine, agriculture, or astronomy—'worked'; what mattered was that they didn't describe objects and laws that had been established as the true basis of reality by Western science.

Colonial assertions of moral and intellectual supremacy over other peoples had the effect of raising both the science and religion of European and Western cultures to a place 'above' the knowledge of other peoples. On one hand this seemed to bolster monotheistic religion, particularly interpretations which saw Christianity as superseding more 'primitive' religions that had come before it and saw an arc of progress in the history of Christian reformation. On the other hand, this concept of social evolution also gave weight to arguments that even reformed Christianity would be superseded by an enlightened secularism. Out of such ideas came the late 19th-century language of science at war with religion, which erupted into social conflicts in several ways. Debates over evolution have long been a staple of these, perhaps most famously in political and legal fights over the teaching of biology in the United States.

The anti-evolution movement from Dayton to design

On 21 March 1925, Austin Peay, the Governor of Tennessee in the United States, put his signature to an Act making it unlawful for teachers to 'teach any theory that denies the story of the Divine Creation of man as taught in the Bible, and to teach instead that man has descended from a lower order of animals'. Other states, including Mississippi and Arkansas, adopted similar anti-evolution measures in the 1920s, but it was in the town of Dayton, Tennessee, that the issue came to a head.

The American Civil Liberties Union (ACLU) saw the Tennessee law as an opportunity to take a stand in defence of intellectual freedom. They placed an advertisement seeking a volunteer to bring a test case. Some of the lawyers and businessmen of Dayton, grasping the opportunity to put their town on the map, persuaded a local science teacher, John Scopes, to put himself forward. What followed generated more publicity than the townsfolk of Dayton could possibly have envisaged.

At first glance, it seems strange that a misdemeanour charge levied against a small-town schoolteacher—for which the maximum penalty was only a small fine—would attract such massive attention. But it was not the legal issue itself, but the opportunity to use the courtroom to debate science and religion that turned the Scopes trial into a public spectacle. Scopes had agreed to stand trial in the hope that (after he was convicted, and had appealed the decision) the US Supreme Court would rule that anti-evolution laws were unconstitutional. With his defence attorneys making no effort to have Scopes acquitted, the trial turned into an internationally discussed drama whose attraction was not a legal question, but philosophical and moral ones. Were evolution and religion compatible? Was it wrong or harmful to teach children that they were descended 'from a lower order of animals'?

The trial's promise of a great debate between science and religion—breathlessly covered in newspapers across the USA and internationally, and taking advantage of new media including cinema newsreels and broadcast radio—also attracted the participation of two of the most famous orators in America: William Jennings Bryan acting for the prosecution, and Clarence Darrow for the defence. Bryan had run three times for president, as the candidate of the Democratic Party, never succeeding. Bryan's support for popular sovereignty against the economic elite had gained him unwavering support in much of the rural United States—especially in regions that felt their way of life threatened by America's rapid urbanization, its increasing industrialization, and those trends' reliance on the nation's diversification through influxes of immigrants. (In the late 19th and early 20th century, the United States welcomed a greater number of immigrants from Europe who were not Protestant, including Jews and Catholics, which gave rise to anti-immigrant sentiment and restriction on migrants enacted in 1924.) Darrow had made his reputation defending politically unpopular clients, including labour union leaders and racial minorities. In 1924, he convinced a judge to withhold the death penalty from two University of Chicago students who had pleaded guilty to abducting and murdering a child.

Although some saw the Scopes trial as a simple confrontation between science and religion, the political speeches made by William Jennings Bryan at the time reveal that the more powerful dynamic was a generally conceived conflict between the fundamentals of Christianity and the evils of the modern world. Bryan was a defender of the newly formed movement for Christian 'fundamentalism'. For the fundamentalists, the spread of Darwinism was both a cause and a symptom of the degeneration of human civilization which they witnessed all around them, from the barbaric violence of the First World War in Europe to the cultural and demographic changes in 1920s America (Figure 7). A new science curriculum that was pushed out across the nation in the 1910s and 1920s had reflected these changes. Not only did many schools teach evolution for the first time; they also emphasized urban hygiene concerns and the industrial uses of science and technology.

Protestant Christianity and a literal reading of the Bible were bulwarks against these developments. Bryan and others feared that teaching children they were animals would brutalize and degrade them:

> Does it not seem a little unfair not to distinguish between man and lower forms of life? What shall we say of the intelligence, not to say religion, of those who are so particular to distinguish between fishes

7. A fundamentalist cartoon from the 1920s depicting the theory of evolution as the tune played by a new 'Pied Piper'—'Science falsely so-called'—stealing away the children of America.

and reptiles and birds, but put a man with an immortal soul in the same circle with the wolf, the hyena and the skunk? What must be the impression made upon children by such a degradation of man?

Bryan and the fundamentalists got what they wanted. In the decades after Scopes was convicted, evolution rarely featured in US classrooms, even in states where it was not illegal. In 1927, the Tennessee Supreme Court overturned Scopes's conviction on a technicality: it should have been the jury and not the judge who had set the amount of the fine. With the ruling, Scopes and the

ACLU no longer had grounds to appeal his conviction and challenge the law itself. It would be another 40 years before an anti-evolution law would finally be challenged in front of the United States Supreme Court.

Creationism, science, and the law

The Establishment Clause of the First Amendment to the US Constitution forbids the government from passing any law 'respecting an establishment of religion'. The original intention was not to exclude religion from public life altogether but to ensure that no particular form of Christianity become an official state-supported religion akin to the Church of England. Participation in public life would not require a 'test' like the requirement to affirm acceptance of the Thirty-Nine Articles of Religion. There was also from the outset a broader hope that this amendment would help to build, in the words of Thomas Jefferson, 'a wall of separation between Church and state'. The enactment of statutes forbidding teachers in state-funded schools from contradicting the 'story of the Divine Creation of man as taught in the Bible' would seem on the face of it to put something of a hole in that wall.

From the middle of the 20th century onwards, the US Supreme Court became increasingly active in applying the Establishment Clause to state-level laws, including those governing schools. State laws allowing time for silent prayer in schools, or for the reading of denominationally neutral prayers, or requiring the Ten Commandments to be posted on classroom walls were all declared unconstitutional. When the US Supreme Court ruled in *Epperson v. Arkansas* (1968) that Arkansas's anti-evolution law (modelled after the 1925 Tennessee law) was unconstitutional, it did so on the grounds that the law gave preference to one religious viewpoint (that saw the Bible as irreconcilable with evolution) over another religious viewpoint (one that interpreted scripture as compatible with Darwinism). The Court declared, in November 1968, that 'fundamentalist sectarian conviction was and is the law's reason for existence'. The *Epperson* case marked the beginning of the legal process which would arbitrate new forms of anti-evolutionism into the 21st century.

In theory, a US state could decide to stop teaching a secular subject in its schools, be it science, history, or literature. But by singling out evolution and by emphasizing the interpretation that Darwinism contradicted the Bible, the courts ruled that the point of Arkansas's anti-evolution law (as was said about Tennessee's in 1925) was to endorse creationism, a religious doctrine.

'Creationism' is a term that has loosely been used to describe religious opposition to a belief in the shared ancestry of different species, including humans. Some creationists may accept gradual evolutionary change within species or closely related families over time (that one original dog kind could evolve into wolves, foxes, Pomeranians, and bloodhounds) but insist that separate divine acts created distinct 'kinds'. This doctrine of separate creations distinguishes creationism from a religious view sometimes called 'theistic evolution': the belief that evolution from a common ancestor was a purposeful, divinely intended, or guided process.

Most creationists base their resistance to evolution at least partly on the authority of their sacred text. The Book of Genesis, for instance, relates that God, over a period of six days, created each kind of living creature separately, made man and woman in his own image, and set them above the rest of creation, before resting on the seventh day. As the King James translation put it:

> And God said, Let us make man in our image, after our likeness: and let them have dominion over the fish of the sea, and over the fowl of the air, and over the cattle, and over all the earth, and over every creeping thing that creepeth upon the earth.

The question of how to interpret sacred texts and to what extent observations of the natural world shape those interpretations has been debated in almost every religious tradition. Creationist religious views typically derive from scriptural accounts of creation whose authorship is held to be divinely inspired or dictated. As we have already seen in the case of arguments about Copernican astronomy, however, it is not easy to specify which parts of the scriptures are to be taken absolutely literally. As William Jennings Bryan explained during the Scopes trial, when the Bible said, 'Ye are the salt of the earth', the text did not mean that 'man was actually salt or that he had flesh of salt, but it is used in the sense of salt as saving God's people'. The term 'literalist' is sometimes used to describe people who believe that a sacred text is entirely true, and that all other knowledge claims must be accommodated to what is given in the text. This does not mean that all literalists agree on what the text means when they read it. At the Scopes trial, Bryan defended the literal truth of the Bible, but admitted that the Bible may have stated those truths in language that even its most devout readers could not interpret with certainty.

What Bryan intended as humility, Darrow attacked as hypocrisy. When the Bible said that the Sun had been stopped in the sky, did that mean that in those days the Sun went round the Earth? No, Bryan said, he believed that the Earth went round the Sun and what the passage meant was that the Earth was stopped in its rotation. Then what about the age of the Earth? Many bibles had the date 4004 BC printed in the margin to indicate the date of creation, as calculated from the text itself. Did Bryan believe the Earth was about 6,000 years old? 'Oh, no; I think it is much older than that.' 'How much?' He could not say. What about the six days of creation in Genesis? Were they 24-hour days? Bryan was clear on that one: 'I do not think they were twenty-four-hour days.' Rather, they were 'periods'. God could have taken six days, six years, six million years, or six hundred million years to create the Earth. 'I do not think it is important whether we believe one or the other,' Bryan said. Soon afterwards, this famous exchange descended into acrimony. Bryan claimed that Darrow was trying to use the courtroom to attack the Bible. Darrow told Bryan he was merely examining 'your fool ideas that no intelligent Christian on Earth believes'.

This famous moment during the Scopes trial reveals two important things about creationism generally. First, even among Christian creationists there has been disagreement about how to interpret Genesis. In the early 20th century, many adopted the 'day-age' interpretation favoured by Bryan according to which each biblical 'day' was in fact a geological 'age' during which many different species were created. Others maintained belief in a very ancient Earth by inferring a long 'gap' between the first moment of creation and the six-day creation of modern Earth and its living species. Within that gap there might have been multiple cataclysms and new creations, responsible for producing the fossil record.

Even before the Scopes trial, creationists sought to use the natural world to justify their biblically derived claims about the age of the world or the creation of species and to raise doubts about Darwinism. The Seventh-Day Adventist geologist George McCready Price was an early and influential example. His *Illogical Geology: The Weakest Point in the Evolution Theory* (1906) and *New Geology* (1923) explained the formation of geological strata and the fossils found within them by arguing that they resulted from a recent universal deluge—which he saw as confirming the biblical account of Noah's flood.

Price's books were an inspiration for the 'creation science' revival of the 1960s and 1970s, led by a Texan Baptist teacher of civil engineering, Henry M. Morris. The Creation Research Society was founded by Morris in 1963, and the Institute for Creation Research in 1970. These promoted a more extreme and allegedly more scientific form of fundamentalist creationism than had ever existed before. As with the anti-evolution campaign of the 1920s, the creation science movement was born of a desire to protect white Christian Americans from modern social changes that they derided as corrosive and degenerate. In 1954, the US Supreme Court ruled that racial segregation in public schools was unconstitutional and creation science flourished at the same time that racial segregationists were decrying the interference of federal courts in local school policies. Like the anti-evolutionists of Bryan's time, creationists in the 1960s attempted to frame the debate over evolution as a moral issue, rather than just one about the scientific or historical truth of the Bible account of creation. The range of evils thought to grow out of a belief in evolution in the 1970s were graphically illustrated in R. G. Elmendorf's 'Evolution Tree', which bore fruit ranging widely from secularism, socialism, and relativism to alcohol, 'dirty books', 'homosex', and even terrorism (Figure 8).

The popularizers of creation science made an attempt to distinguish it from the earlier creationism of Bryan and Scopes-era anti-evolutionists. Creation *science*, they argued, was not a religious doctrine per se. It observed nature and sought to confirm theories about the natural world. That those theories were inspired by biblical accounts of creation did not, they argued, make the scientific evidence for those theories religious. This argument had legal ramifications. The US Constitution might prohibit teaching religion, but says nothing about what kinds of science may be taught.

Soon after the State of Arkansas lost the *Epperson* case and had to abandon its anti-evolution law, it enacted a new statute requiring 'balanced treatment' between 'evolution science' and 'creation science' According to the law:

Creation-science includes the scientific evidences and related inferences that indicate: (1) Sudden creation of the universe, energy,

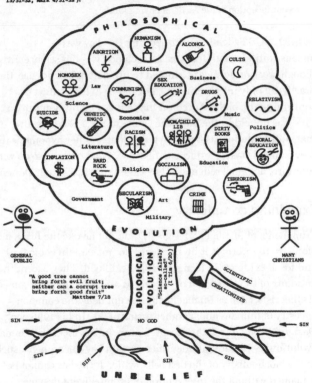

8. A creationist image of the 1970s: the 'Evolution Tree' is nourished by sin and unbelief, and its fruits include a range of secular ideologies, immoral activities, and economic and social evils.

and life from nothing; (2) The insufficiency of mutation and natural selection in bringing about development of all living kinds from a single organism; (3) Changes only within fixed limits of originally created kinds of plants and animals; (4) Separate ancestry for man and apes; (5) Explanation of the earth's geology by catastrophism, including the occurrence of a worldwide flood; and (6) A relatively recent inception of the earth and living kinds.

In 1982, a US Federal Court ruled that this law was unconstitutional and that 'creation science' was not science. Even though creation science attempted to use nature as evidence, the practice of only interpreting such evidence in the context of confirming the biblical account made it a religious enterprise. This was upheld by the Supreme Court in 1987. Not long after that, anti-evolutionists began to talk about another hypothesis that they claimed was scientific and, because it had nothing to do with scripture, not at all religious. They called this 'Intelligent Design'.

Explaining complexity

Proponents of intelligent design (ID) do not invoke the Bible, let alone try to interpret it literally, and do not explain geological and fossil evidence in terms of a biblical flood. They accept the antiquity of the Earth and of humanity, and, in the case of some ID theorists, such as Michael Behe, do not deny the common ancestry of humans and all other forms of life. In his 1996 book *Darwin's Black Box*, Behe accepted more or less all of the standard evolutionary picture but identifies certain key phenomena, such as the biochemistry of the first cells, which he insists cannot be explained without the intervention of an intelligent designer. Structures like the flagellum, a tail-like mechanism that allows some bacteria to move, exhibit 'irreducible complexity'. It could not have evolved gradually because without all of its several pieces working together, it would not provide an evolutionary advantage. Thus, it must have been created all at once.

Arguments about 'irreducible complexity' are a new form of a very old anti-Darwinian argument, namely that complex structures could not have evolved by natural selection because the intermediate forms containing only some of the parts would not have been adaptive. What use is a part of an eye, half a wing, or three-quarters of a flagellum? In general terms, evolutionists have been able to answer this objection by finding, either in fossils or in living species, evidence of intermediate structures that did exist and were in fact adaptive. In the case of the eye, Darwin himself listed various forms of eyes, from a small patch of light-sensitive cells to the complex 'camera' eyes of humans and other animals, showing how each was adaptive and could have evolved into the next in the series. Scientists now estimate that this entire evolutionary process could even have been achieved within a mere half a million years.

Advantages were also conferred by the precursors to fully fledged wings. Feathers, for instance, seem first to have evolved as a form of insulation before being co-opted by natural selection to aid a quite different function—flight. It is harder to produce these scenarios in the case of biochemistry because chemical reactions, unlike feathers, do not fossilize. However, using evidence from currently living species it is possible to reconstruct evolutionary scenarios. This has been done, for instance, in the case of the famous bacterial flagellum, which, it has been suggested, evolved through the co-option of a very similar existing structure used by bacteria for injecting toxic proteins into the cells of their hosts. So the answer to the question, 'What use is a part of an eye, half a wing, or three-quarters of a flagellum?', is 'Light-detection, warmth, and toxin-injection, respectively.'

Some accounts of ID rely upon negative argumentation. They argue that Darwinian natural selection is wrong, or, more often, insufficient to explain nature. Critics sometimes claim that this is simply the 'God of the Gaps' argument refurbished for the age of molecular biology. In other instances, ID arguments look like appeals to the wonderfulness of nature familiar from older natural theology texts, albeit with more modern examples.

When ID advocates first sought to argue for inclusion of their ideas in schools, they tended to mention a 'designer' and 'intelligence', but avoided addressing questions about whether the designer was God, whether there were one or many designers, or how an idea in the mind of some intelligence became manifested in the physical world of matter. This was necessary in order to make the case that ID was 'science' and not 'religion' within the dichotomy that the courts had effectively turned into precedent in the earlier creationism cases.

The first court challenge to ID came after a school board in Dover, Pennsylvania, adopted a rule in October 2004 requiring students to be read a statement asserting that 'Gaps in the [evolution] Theory exist for which there is no evidence' and telling them that 'Intelligent design is an explanation of the origin of life that differs from Darwin's view.' In the lawsuit that followed, Judge John E. Jones III ruled that intelligent design is not a science. Despite its lack of explicit theological conclusions about the Bible or the age of the world, its insistence on supernatural causation disqualified it as science. Based in part on the conclusion that ID is not science, Jones ruled that promoting it represented an endorsement of religion. The historical connection between ID and other forms of anti-evolution also factored into the judge's opinion. Trial testimony revealed that the publishers of the intelligent design textbook *Of Pandas and People* had originally prepared the book about 'creation science' and had simply substituted the phrase 'intelligent design' after the Supreme Court ruling in 1987.

By the 1990s, biblical anti-evolution laws had been declared unconstitutional; laws requiring 'balanced treatment' for evolution and 'creation science' had gone the same way; but opinion polls continued to find that between 45 and 50 per cent of the population of the USA believed that human beings were created by God in their present form at some time in the last 10,000 years. (This figure is about 40 per cent in most recent polls, with most of the rest of the population believing that humanity evolved through an evolutionary process somehow guided by God.)

Since the Dover trial ended in 2005, anti-evolution-minded school boards and politicians have shifted away from promoting specific forms of anti-evolution alternatives and instead emphasize the 'academic freedom' of teachers to teach what they believe to be true or the religious freedom of teachers and students to have their viewpoints included. The Louisiana Science Education Act of 2008 is the most politically successful of these efforts. The law was based upon language drafted by the Discovery Institute, a think tank that has spent millions of dollars to try to create political, scientific, and legal legitimacy for intelligent design.

At the Dover trial, witnesses compared ID to Paley's *Natural Theology*. While the two share superficial similarities, they're actually very different. Paley's insistence that evidence for divine design is found in objects being well adapted to natural laws is almost exactly the opposite of an argument that claims that intelligent design is found in the phenomena where natural laws are not enough. Given the theological vagueness of most ID, it may be surprising that the movement has found strong appeal among evangelical Protestants who endorse a literal reading of the Bible. In light of the larger cultural anxieties that the evolution debate in America evokes, support for ID and other forms of creationism are more comprehensible.

But is it science?

US courts have ruled that creation science and ID are not actually science. This raises complex questions of how one distinguishes between science and non-science, and whether it's the case that everything that is religious is non-scientific or vice versa. There are various candidates for such 'demarcation criteria'. Some say that true science must be empirically testable, others that it must make 'falsifiable' claims, others that it must offer explanations only in terms of natural laws and natural processes.

Philosophers of science are much less optimistic than they were a few decades ago about the possibility of finding any complete and coherent demarcation criteria. It is accepted that many scientific claims—including many of the most interesting ones—are not directly empirically testable but only become so as part of a complex network of auxiliary theoretical assumptions and scientific instruments. For instance, a mathematical model of the Big Bang cannot be tested by direct observation, but only indirectly through predictions about the behaviour of measuring apparatus when a particular reaction is set off in a massive particle accelerator. On the other hand, creation scientists made very clearly testable claims about the age of the Earth and the separate ancestry of all species.

It is also accepted that good scientists will often hold on to their theories in the face of inconsistent empirical evidence and seek to reinterpret that evidence rather than declare their theory 'falsified'. Some philosophers speak instead of the 'robustness' of theories which can generally overcome apparent inconsistencies and can explain a wide range of observed phenomena. The modern framework of evolutionary theory successfully explains and unifies a huge body of evidence accumulated and interpreted over many generations. It makes sense of the fossil record, the geographical distribution of species, the physical similarities between related plants and animals, and the vestigial organs that testify to earlier evolutionary forms. Recent advances in genetic sequencing have provided a huge new mass of evidence which confirms evolutionary theory while identifying a whole new range of puzzles and anomalies. In the face of puzzles and anomalies a good scientist, especially when working with such a well-confirmed theory, does not declare their theory falsified, but designs new experiments and develops new theoretical models to solve those puzzles and resolve those anomalies. This model relies on the good faith of a scientific community; that their decisions to solve puzzles or to alter their hypotheses are taken without regard for political, cultural, or financial considerations. As we shall see in Chapter 6, some forms of science denial abuse that good faith.

Evolution worldwide

In the English-speaking world, debates over evolution and religion have often centred upon Christianity. This is perhaps unsurprising since this was the world that Darwin himself came from and most closely influenced. The experiences of other cultures and religions with evolution have been shaped by their encounter with both the idea of evolution and the people who introduced it.

One month after Darwin's and Wallace's theory of species change was read before the Linnaean Society of London, the British parliament, meeting a mile away, voted to grant Queen Victoria sovereign authority over India. Although the British colonial presence in India had already been felt for centuries, the consolidation of imperial control under the Crown coinciding with the rise of evolution as the intellectual framework to interpret nature and progress influenced the way that colonized Indians experienced Darwinism, and the twinned concepts of science and religion.

As historian Peter Gottschalk relates in his study of science and religion in colonial India, people there had various systems of observing and interpreting the world around them, and applying that knowledge to practice long before European imperialism. What British colonizers brought with them were their own systems of categorizing different kinds of knowledge, and a demand to align beliefs, practices, and explanations that they encountered with the ones they had developed at home. Just as domestic British society had experienced debates and wars over church authority, toleration, and political participation by requiring very explicit distinctions between people by religion, colonial efforts to administrate also involved efforts to classify everyone by religious identity. 'The modern view of India as a primarily religious country, insolvably split between Hindus and Muslims,' Gottschalk observes, 'worked within a system of knowledge largely shaped by models originating in the West and generally controlled by Westerners.'

Some scholars of Indian religion go so far as to say that British imperialism 'invented' India's most populous religion, Hinduism. By this they don't mean that British colonizers came up with the texts, beliefs, and practices of people, most of which pre-date the colonial age by many centuries. Instead they mean that the British imperial view of Indian people created a singular category of 'Hindu' to describe a wide range of such beliefs and practices largely defined by contrast to Muslims and Sikhs. Debate about this supposed invention of Hinduism has divided scholars for decades, and has taken on political importance in India itself, where claims of the unity and antiquity of Hinduism shape some interpretations of national identity. These controversies are rooted in British and other European concepts of religion that in colonial times were often defined by their distinction from science and rationality. These definitions were tools of colonial control, as they served to allow British colonizers in India to treat indigenous forms of knowledge as less evolved than their own.

Indians' engagement with European concepts of science, imposed by colonial power, affected the way that Darwin's ideas of evolution were interpreted. Race and racism figured substantially in this. Interpretations of Darwin were frequently used to justify a hierarchy of races, which British administrators and naturalists used in conjunction with their interpretation of religious 'caste' to create hierarchies among Indians. For example, T. H. Huxley argued that different Hindu castes had resulted from different proportions of racial mixing.

Among Hindus today, there is a range of interpretations of evolution, with a much higher proportion of Hindus in India responding that they accept an evolutionary account of species change than the proportion of Protestants who do in the United States. Many point out that Hindu cosmology has no difficulty accepting an Earth that is billions of years old. (In fact, some interpretations of the *Rig Veda* date the Earth as over 8 billion years old, nearly twice the scientifically accepted age of about 4.5 billion.) Several Hindu texts speak of a series of incarnations of the god Vishnu in different animal, animal–human, and then human forms in a progression of complexity that many consider to parallel the emergence of more complex species in Darwinian evolution. While this is not the same thing as saying that ancient Hindu scriptures anticipated natural selection, this is often cited to support claims that Hinduism is not in conflict with evolutionary science.

This is not to suggest that all Hindus find evolution compatible with their religious belief, but to observe that acceptance or rejection of the theory is conditioned by the colonial and post-colonial authority of science. Arguing that Hinduism is inherently compatible with science has been one way in which the formerly colonized Hindu people of India translate their own intellectual and religious heritage into the modern frameworks that hold science up as a uniquely valid form of knowledge.

For some groups of colonized and marginalized peoples, the use of science as a tool of hegemonic power and the way that colonizers used dualistic concepts of science and religion to categorize and evaluate indigenous knowledge has created wariness of the scientific claims and the validity of the knowledge it creates. Scepticism about evolution, even when articulated in ways that contrast it with traditional beliefs about the origin of humanity or the creation and age of the Earth, should therefore be regarded differently when looking outside the Christian European context in which Darwin and his contemporaries worked.

A telling example of this is among Native American peoples who have frequently been used as objects of scientific study. As Kim TallBear observes, knowledge about human evolution and theories of race ancestry often made use of the first human inhabitants of the Americas, often without their consent. European colonizers used Native American bodies, blood, and other artefacts to create knowledge about race that they then used to justify the dispossession of indigenous peoples. That colonial project was aided by the use of scientific narratives to replace indigenous cultural histories with accounts of people and their past that they had no say in creating. Several years after some members of the Havasupai tribe (native to the Grand Canyon of Arizona) allowed the collection of blood samples to research high incidents of diabetes among their people, it came to light that scientists had continued to use these samples for other purposes without consent, including research into the genetic origins of the Havasupai people (which not only contradicted their creation narratives, but which could be used to question their territorial claims). As TallBear concludes of indigenous critics of evolutionary sciences, 'to characterize them as simply anti-science, or as religious zealots not only misses their sophisticated historical analyses and political insights, but misunderstands indigenous creationism as no different from the type of Christian creationism currently challenging the biological sciences and school curriculums.'

Around the world, in the past and today, the ways that scientific and religious ideas affect people cannot be separated from who they are: their own identity, history, and culture. One reason why evolution has remained a central issue in the science and religion story for so long is that it transforms those very issues, raising questions about how we understand our human selves, the origins of our societies, and how we act and interact with one another.

Chapter 5
Mind, brain, and morality

Perhaps the most important reason that evolution has been more controversial than many other scientific topics has to do with the implication that it provides a biological and historical account of what it means to be human. It speaks to a deeper concern over what we are as human beings, whether our bodies and minds define us, whether our selves change over the course of our lives, and whether anything exists as fundamentally 'us' after our bodies cease to function. If we are defined by our biology, by the genes and evolutionary processes that determine how our brains think and control our actions, what place is there for morality?

Since the 19th century, scientific studies of mind, brain, and morality have been providing challenges to religious ideas about identity and ethics. What if the part of the self we call the 'soul' is merely a by-product of chemical and electrical brain activity? If people's actions are a combination of genetics, brain activity, and social and cultural conditioning, what place does such a view leave for belief in moral responsibility in this life or the prospect of rewards or punishments in the next?

For many people, these questions about mind and morality drive the whole debate about science and religion. As in other areas of theology, so in ethics, some look to revelation or a sacred text for answers, while others look to human instincts or moral sentiments, and yet others look to the natural world around them (or some combination of all of these). Many believers resist the idea that human consciousness, morality, and even religion itself can be explained scientifically. If religious experience and human morality can be explained as natural phenomena, there seems to be no further need for supernatural accounts of such things.

Consider the famous and extraordinary case of Phineas Gage. In 1848, Gage was a railroad construction worker when a dynamite accident propelled a metre-long iron tamping rod through his cheek and out of the top of his head (Figure 9). Astonishingly, Gage survived. But it soon became clear that the damage to the frontal lobes of his brain had altered his personality. He had lost the ability to empathize with others, and his social behaviour became unpredictable and erratic. Accounts of people like Gage spurred interest in the brain and its role in making people act in certain ways, leading to new fields of scientific research into the relationship between our mental and physical selves.

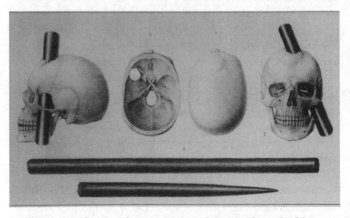

9. Illustration showing the tamping iron that went through Phineas Gage's head in 1848, and the route that it took through his skull.

Brain and mind

Nineteenth-century attempts to specify the exact nature of the connection between brain and mind saw the emergence of the science of 'craniology' or 'phrenology', according to which the extent of the development of different sections of the brain could be discerned from the shape of someone's skull. The different parts of the brain under the 'bumps' on the skull were correlated with different mental traits, such as love of children, secretiveness, self-esteem, and so on. Phrenologists could thus tell people what the shape of their head revealed about their mental capacities. It became a popular craze for a while in Victorian Britain. People were eagerly told what their skulls revealed about their character traits and their future destinies, by those with a special understanding of the secret workings of nature. Queen Victoria even arranged phrenological readings for her children. Some phrenologists of the era claimed that diagnosing mental traits was essential to helping people improve themselves morally. Thus, they presented phrenology as a respectable science that helped create an ethical society aligned with religious values.

At the same time, phrenology and other 19th-century efforts to study the brain and skull were used to make claims of gendered and racial differences in intelligence, and thus to justify the political inequalities of the day. Most famously, in the 1830s and 1840s the American natural historian Samuel George Morton acquired a large collection of skulls from different cultures and regions of the world, and concluded that different races had been separately created by God with varying abilities of mind and body. Morton's comparisons of European-American and African-American skulls in particular were cited to justify the continued practice of slavery in the United States.

Although in many ways phrenology was wrong-headed, the basic idea that different mental functions correlated with particular parts of the brain turned out to be fruitful. Studying patients who had suffered brain damage, scientists started making more informed statements about localization. In the 1860s, the French physician Paul Broca discovered the area—still known as 'Broca's area'—in the frontal lobes of the brain that was responsible for speech production. The more recent invention of brain-scanning technologies has allowed this project to be pursued with greater precision, revealing the dynamic interactions of different parts of the brain, and offering insights into the working of intact brains as well as damaged ones. Neuroscientists can even stimulate parts of the brain experimentally and study the mental effects on their intrepid subjects. These techniques have all been applied specifically to religious experiences as well as to many other mental capacities. A study of Carmelite nuns carried out in 2006 by Mario Beauregard and Vincent Paquette, for example, identified different brain areas that were activated during their spiritual experiences.

Dualism and physicalism

What are the implications of this scientific research for religion? One newspaper report of Beauregard and Paquette's study ran under the headline: 'Nuns Prove God Is Not Figment of the Mind'. The somewhat tortuous idea behind the headline seemed to be that if the whole brain is involved in religious experiences then that contradicts the theory that there is one special 'God spot', perhaps in the temporal lobes, and with it the associated belief that religious experiences are 'nothing but' the activation of that one brain area. Why it would be any less religiously or theologically troubling to find that spiritual feelings were produced by the activation of many parts of the brain, rather than just one, is not clear. This is a good example of the theological and philosophical ambiguity of empirical neuroscientific studies.

Since the 1980s, there have been several studies which use functional Magnetic Resonance Imaging (fMRI) to study the brains of Buddhist monks during periods of meditation (Figure 10). Some results from these studies suggest that 'expert meditators' develop certain cognitive abilities through repeated practice—including sensory processing and mathematical abilities. Public interest in these studies has coincided with increased interest in recreating the effects of these meditative practices—under the general banner of 'mindfulness'—without necessarily understanding the spiritual and supernatural explanations that Buddhists have traditionally used to explain their own experiences of meditation.

However, some Buddhist groups have embraced this scientific reinterpretation of millennia-old practices and have encouraged it. The Dalai Lama, leader of a Tibetan Buddhist movement, has been a strong supporter of neuroscientific research on Buddhist meditation and encouraged his followers to participate in fMRI studies. His engagement with science in this way has not been without controversy. Some scientists have protested his speaking at neuroscience conferences, claiming that inviting him promotes

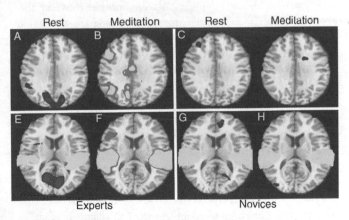

10. Figure from a 2008 research paper studying the effects of meditation on neurological states. The article concludes that 'expert meditators' with more than 10,000 hours experience in Buddhist meditation show different brain activity than 'novice meditators'.

religion in what should be a secular setting. Some critics claim that these efforts are an attempt to co-opt science's cultural prestige to bring attention and credibility to political movements for Tibetan sovereignty, implying parallels between repression of Tibet and repression of science itself. In part because of his efforts to promote this harmony between Buddhism and neuroscience, and to see science as legitimizing religious experience rather than superseding it, the Dalai Lama was awarded the Templeton Prize in 2012.

The success of neuroscience in showing that there are correlations between certain states of the brain and certain mental experiences, including religious ones, has been interpreted by some as a direct refutation of traditional beliefs about mystical experiences and the immortality of the soul. According to this sceptical stance, an experience can be caused by the brain or by an immaterial being (God or the soul) but not both: a neurological explanation of an experience rules out a supernatural or religious one. Science has explained away the supernatural. That might seem a reasonable and simple enough assumption. However, there are plenty of philosophers, scientists, and theologians who would deny it. To offer neurological or, for that matter, evolutionary explanations of where our religious and moral beliefs come from is an interesting scientific enterprise. It flourishes today as one part of the ambitious programme of research known as 'cognitive science'. But since absolutely all our beliefs—religious, scientific, or otherwise—are, on this hypothesis, the products of the same evolved neurological apparatus, drawing attention to that fact does not get us any further forward in the philosophical endeavour of distinguishing between the true ones and the false ones.

Another response to the perceived challenge of neuroscience to religious belief has been to adopt a form of 'dualism'—in other words, to assert that there exist two distinct kinds of substance, or properties, the mental and the physical, which interact with each other, especially in human beings. The dualist would interpret the close correlations discovered by neuroscientists not as evidence that the mind is nothing but brain activity, but rather that the mind interacts with the brain, or uses the brain as its instrument. René Descartes's 17th-century version of this philosophy is the one that has received most scholarly attention, but there are plenty of modern successors to his view, both among philosophers and more widely. Key problems in making sense of dualism include the question of how the physical and the non-physical can causally interact with each other, and explaining why dualism is to be preferred to the apparently simpler alternative of physicalism, according to which mental properties are properties of the brain.

Even if all mental experience is, in some sense, physical, it is still not straightforward to articulate what that sense is. Why is it that particular bits of matter (exclusively, as far as we know, complex networks of nerve cells within the brains of living animals) exhibit the properties of consciousness and others (such as rocks, vegetables, or even computers) do not? Philosophers and theologians interested in this question have discussed concepts such as 'emergence', 'supervenience', and 'non-reductive physicalism', all of which try to articulate how mental realities can be both dependent on and yet autonomous from the physical. To say that the mind is 'emergent' or 'supervenient' is to suggest it is autonomous, not in the sense of being able to exist independently of the brain, but in the sense that it exhibits properties and regularities that are not susceptible to systematic reduction to the neurological level.

In a somewhat different way, social scientists also point to culture as an emergent phenomenon that can't be determined at a purely neurological level. Morality exists as a shared set of norms and practices rooted in a common experience among people in a society. Such an account does not easily answer the question of whether the moral values of a society are 'good' in any absolute or objective sense. But these accounts explain why communities are aligned by shared values and why they respond to perceived deviance in the ways that they do. From this perspective, it is the belief in some immaterial part of oneself, and in a system of rewards and punishments, rather than the reality of that world-view, that explains why people seek to act morally.

Selfishness and altruism

When freethinking and anti-Christian works such as Thomas Paine's *Age of Reason* (1794) started to become more widely available, one of the leading concerns of the faithful was that if people ceased to believe in heaven and hell, then they would feel free to indulge their most sensual passions and selfish appetites. Without religion, it was feared, human society would descend into animalistic anarchy. As one judge said when sentencing a London bookseller to imprisonment for selling Paine's works, if these books were widely read and believed then the law would be deprived of 'one of its principal sanctions—the dread of future punishments'.

This same logic, that denying immortality would lead to immorality, was what drove William Jennings Bryan's movement to halt the teaching of evolution in the 1920s. Many today still echo the sentiments of this 18th-century judge and argue that religious beliefs are necessary to provide moral guidance and standards of virtuous conduct in an otherwise corrupt, materialistic, and degenerate world. Religions certainly do provide a framework within which people can learn the difference between right and wrong. An individual might consult the scriptures to discover that God has told his people to be truthful, faithful, and respectful towards their parents; and not to steal, nor commit adultery, nor worship false gods. Believers can also hope to receive moral guidance from the voice of God within, in the form of their conscience. If they follow the divine path faithfully, they will be deemed to be among the righteous rather than the wicked at the day of judgement. The unbeliever, in contrast, is supposed to be a sensuous, self-indulgent, selfish creature whose motto is 'Let us eat and drink; for tomorrow we die.'

The alleged connection between unbelief and selfishness has been strengthened by a particular interpretation of evolution as a process driven by self-assertion and competition. Standard explanations of evolution have emphasized the fact that a trait or behaviour cannot evolve unless it is for the good of the individual organism. This would seem to rule out the possibility of altruism (except as a sort of enlightened self-interest). If evolution cannot produce genuine altruism, then perhaps the only explanation for the self-sacrifice displayed by saintly individuals is that they are inspired or empowered by God. Even the former director of the Human Genome Project (and 2020 Templeton Prize winner) Francis Collins suggests in his book *The Language of God* (2006) that the existence of the 'moral law' of love and altruism within every human heart cannot be explained by science alone.

Others seeking natural explanations for altruism, selflessness, and moral behaviour have turned to evolution. Some interpretations of evolution seem to suggest that selfish behaviour that increases the likelihood of reproducing will be retained by the process of natural selection. For the arch-atheist science writer Richard Dawkins, author of *The Selfish Gene* (1976), it was not individual organisms, but genes themselves that exhibited this tendency to value their own reproduction, and which he described as 'selfish' in an extended and metaphorical sense. A year earlier, in 1975, biologist E. O. Wilson had published *Sociobiology: The New Synthesis*, which looked to group-selection rather than gene-selection to provide an explanation. Wilson argued that groups evolve to have certain behaviours that may not be beneficial to the individual, but which ensure greater survival and success for the overall group. Such explanations don't explain instincts and behaviours in terms of whether they are morally good or bad, but on whether they contribute to the overall fitness of a community who practises them. This kind of group-level thinking about evolution provides one way of thinking about human behaviours that don't seem to immediately benefit the individual.

Dealing with deviance

The moral and legal codes of the monotheistic traditions reveal preoccupations with all sorts of different social problems, including how to get on with neighbouring tribes, how to deal with religious dissent, how to enforce regulations relating to many details of everyday life including diet, dress, and domestic arrangements, and how to punish those who break the rules. One set of concerns that recurs frequently relates to sex, sexuality, and gender expression. Sexual desire has produced as much conflict and anxiety as it has pleasure for as long as human civilizations have existed. And many religions dictate rules and regulations to cope with this very powerful human drive. Generally speaking, sex between men and women, within marriage, to produce children, has been approved of (although St Paul thought it was better to remain completely celibate while awaiting the imminent final judgement), while virtually any other kind of sex, most notably sex with oneself, or with someone of the same sex, or with someone in one's own family, has normally been condemned.

In addition to regarding some forms of sexuality as deviant, many religious groups enforce strictly defined gender norms—including prescriptions on dress, rules regarding access to certain religious rituals or offices, even insisting upon the inequality of partners within marriage. Some religious groups draw upon scriptural language to justify equating gender identity with the sexual characteristics of one's body and insisting upon strict binaries between men and women. Other religious communities, including some forms of Hinduism and some indigenous American societies, have long-standing traditions of a 'third gender' or non-binary conception of gender that pre-date modern scientific interpretations of gender and sexual identity. This complex view of gender is not restricted to humans. The Hindu deity Arthanariswara is depicted as half-man, half-woman.

In modern societies where science and medicine have gradually taken over from traditional religious beliefs as the most acceptable sources of publicly agreed distinctions between the normal and the deviant, two parallel trends can be discerned: a de-moralization of previously moral issues, but also a concomitant medical and scientific imposition, reinforcement, and naturalization of existing social divisions and inequalities. Modern science has proved just as ideologically malleable as the Bible when it comes to arguing either for or against such divisions. As we have seen with historical debates about racism and colonialism, scientific and religious arguments have similarly been invoked to justify a range of interpretations regarding sex, gender, and identity.

The naturalistic fallacy

Science and religion have both been used in pursuit of all sorts of different political goals. Neither is inherently liberal or conservative, racist or egalitarian, repressive or permissive. Each provides a way of understanding the world which might be made consilient with almost any ideological vision. But while we are used to the idea that religious believers will look at ethical and political questions through the lenses of their particular faith commitments, we have not yet learned to be quite so attentive in the case of those who claim to speak for science. On the face of it, a scientific approach to ethics promises to be a balanced and objective one—and one which takes its lead from nature rather than from human prejudices. Does nature not speak with a clear and impartial voice?

Some philosophers, driven by the desire to develop a more scientific approach to morality, have constructed whole systems of 'evolutionary ethics'. For such thinkers, the fact that humanity's conscience and moral feelings are the product of evolution requires that ethics should be understood from an evolutionary rather than a religious or even a philosophical point of view. The problem that all such schemes encounter is that there is more to ethics than following nature. Even if it can be shown that we are endowed with a particular 'natural' instinct by our evolutionary history, that observation does not get us any closer to answering the ethical question of whether it is right to follow that instinct. Presumably the instincts that incline people towards violence, theft, and adultery have evolutionary origins too. Whichever interpretation of evolutionary biology we care to endorse, it is perfectly clear (as it has been to moral philosophers through the ages) that human beings are born with the propensity both to seek their own good and also the good of (at least some) others. The question of whether the altruistic instinct, for instance, is a natural one is completely separate from the question of whether it is one that we should follow, and to what extent. That question will be answered only by thinking about the rules and goals according to which we, individually and communally, wish to live our lives.

The natural theologians of centuries past had justification for this. They reasoned that morality was reflected in the natural word because of the benevolence of the God who created it. But without presupposing divine goodness, inferences from natural facts to moral truths no longer seem so logical. The mistake of supposing that something is ethically desirable just because it can be shown to be natural, or evolved, is sometimes referred to as the 'naturalistic fallacy'. This strange phrase is taken from the English philosopher G. E. Moore's 1903 book *Principia ethica*. Here Moore stated that any system of ethics which tried, misguidedly as he thought, to define the ethical predicate 'good' in terms of a naturalistic predicate such as 'pleasurable' or 'useful' or 'for the good of the species' was guilty of committing the 'naturalistic fallacy'.

Some religious thinkers have invoked the 'naturalistic fallacy' as a reason to resist all secular and scientific approaches to ethics. However, it should be pointed out that Moore's ban on translating the word 'good' into any non-ethical term was applied by him to metaphysical and philosophical systems of ethics too. In fact, Moore's view really amounted to complete moral mysticism. A system of ethics which identifies 'good' with 'in accordance with God's will' or 'for the greatest good of the greatest number', or anything else at all (apart from Moore's own favoured sense of goodness as an intuited quality of beauty) is equally guilty of committing the 'naturalistic fallacy'. From this point of view, religious and scientific approaches to ethics are each in an equally bad position.

Beyond nature

Recent debates about science and ethics have often proceeded as if moral goodness and altruism were synonymous. Some claim that altruism is natural and so we should follow nature. Others insist that we have evolved to be essentially selfish and so we need to struggle against nature. But both views are based on a very limited understanding of what it is to live a good life. Individualism and self-development have traditionally been valued by both secular and religious moralists. As several commentators have pointed out, when Jesus told the rich young man to sell all his possessions and give the proceeds to the poor so that he might have 'treasure in heaven', that advice was given for the good of the young man, not for the good of the poor. There are political connotations too. The ideology of altruism is one that is open to manipulation by ruling elites. The idea of living for others sounds like a noble one. But it can be used both by totalitarian governments seeking to persuade their subjects that the interests of the whole must come before their own individual rights, and also by public leaders who may exploit the good will and generosity of their supporters to serve their own aims. Again, the value of altruism is something to be decided by political and moral discussion, not by an appeal to nature.

As any practical discussion of moral values becomes inseparable from the political realities in which those values will be invoked, another sense of identity must come into the conversation in addition to the mind, soul, and brain. Our human selves are shaped by social factors that do not necessarily exist in our genes or brains, but are emergent properties of the societies that we are born into, complete with histories, cultures, and other contexts. Even though concepts like 'race' or nationality may not exist as purely biological phenomena, they exist as social factors that impact who we are just as our bodies and minds do.

Philosophers of science have also observed that these kinds of social realities impact the nature of scientific enquiry itself, and even call into question whether scientists can obtain a kind of 'objective' truth independent of cultural biases or moral values. Since the 1980s, feminist epistemology of science has raised questions about what Donna Haraway refers to as 'situated knowledge' in science: that access to knowledge about nature and the ability to make claims about knowledge are shaped not just by the natural world scientists observe but also by their relationships to other knowers, their embodiment, and social status. These concepts have not only shaped how philosophers and other scholars view the practice of science but also the relationship of its knowledge claims to other systems, including religious ones.

In the modern world, it seems as though science, technology, and medicine increasingly dominate attempts to make moral meanings. For much of the 19th and early 20th centuries, scientific visions of the future were often laced with optimism, and a belief in progress and improved human flourishing. Visions of people travelling through space, of cheap and clean energy, of cures to all major diseases, were common themes of science fiction and of speculative portrayals of the world of tomorrow. If moral crises were triggered by wars, scarcity of food and natural resources, and economic inequality, science and technology could solve those problems and open up a world where moral behaviour was made easier. But in recent decades, scientific optimism has given way to realities that sound as darkly apocalyptic as some visions from revelation.

Instead of being warned by the great religious prophets of the past that we must mend our wicked ways or face the wrath of God and cosmic cataclysms, we are now warned that our social behaviour, gluttony, and greed will spread disease, result in obesity, and lead to the flooding, burning, and destruction of our planet as a result of catastrophic levels of global warming. And the age of Covid-19 has illustrated moral questions about selfishness and altruism in concrete ways. The details have changed, and of course these projections of future disaster are based on scientific evidence, but the structure of the argument remains the same. Science and medicine now provide us with frightening visions of the future which policy-makers and political leaders use to try to persuade us, as did the prophets of old, to repent and change our ways before it is too late. Whatever our views about morality, it is hopefully clear by now that there is no straight path from either religion or science to simple ethical pronouncements. We should be sceptical of a political figure claiming they are 'following the science' just as we might be of a religious demagogue claiming they are following the will of God. There are no shortcuts in the complex and communal worlds of ethics, identity, and politics.

Chapter 6
The worlds of science and religion

In Hawaii on 17 July 2019, 38 elders went down on their knees. Along with hundreds of other protesters, they blocked a road leading up a mountain. The mountain in question was Maunakea. Its name is a contraction of 'Mauna a Wākea', meaning the birthplace of the god Wākea. The elders were the first to be arrested during protests to prevent construction of a scientific instrument known as the Thirty Meter Telescope (TMT) (Figure 11).

In the four centuries since Galileo turned his telescope skyward, the science of astronomy has expanded beyond measure. Earth- and space-based telescopes have empowered astronomers to see phenomena in increasingly detailed resolution, observe wavelengths outside the limits of human vision, and penetrate into far greater distances beyond the Earth. Because of the finite speed at which light travels, the ability to see across intergalactic distances in space corresponds to looking 'backwards in time'—making it possible for scientists to construct their own account of the beginnings of the universe, trying to describe what could have happened in the earliest moments after an initial Big Bang approximately 14 billion years ago.

At a basic level, modern telescopes function in much the same way as Galileo's: optical tools collect and focus electromagnetic waves

5. INCLUDING BUILDINGS, STRUCTURES AND FACILITIES SHALL BE COMPATIBLE WITH THE LOCALITY AND SURROUNDING AREAS APPROPRIATE TO THE PHYSICAL CONDITIONS AND CAPABILITIES OF THE SPECIFIC PARCEL(S); AND

6. THE EXISTING PHYICAL AND ENVIRONMEN ASPECTS OF THE LAND, SUCH AS NATURAL BEAU AND OPEN SPACE CHAR ERISTICS WILL BE PRES

11. A 2014 photograph from protests against the building of the Thirty Meter Telescope in Hawaii. Advocates of the TMT have often dismissed the concerns of protesters as 'religious'.

(visible light, X-rays, microwaves, or radio waves, for example). But the images we 'see' could never be observed with unaided eyes, even if we were somehow transported to the right vantage point. These images are composites of data that have no direct visual counterpart. Telescopes are calibrated to record variations in electromagnetic signals and data is filtered and analysed according to mathematical models that factor in assumptions about how light, gravity, mass, and space all function over large distances and timescales. With each new 'discovery' made by these telescopes, debates about realism—about the existence of apparently 'unobservable' things like black holes, exoplanets, dark matter, and dark energy—are reopened and re-examined. The 2015 discovery of gravitational waves (fluctuations in space and time caused by accelerating masses) has made possible a new form of telescope—one that does not rely upon electromagnetic waves.

Also different from Galileo's time, no one person could design, build, or operate today's advanced telescopes. From casting and polishing mirrors, to writing computer code for rapid adjusting for fluctuations in the air, to manufacturing the housing to hold and aim the device, to rendering a widely published image, a 'telescope' is a complex combination of technologies. Thirty metres refers to the diameter of the telescope's primary mirror, but overall, the TMT design calls for a telescope 55 metres wide and 50 metres tall housed in a building that would be by far the largest structure on Maunakea. Modern telescopes represent a major investment of time and money. Like many large-scale observatories and laboratories, the TMT is also a product of international collaboration (including the USA, China, India, Canada, and Japan), both a product and a tool of modern diplomacy and state power as well as science.

Advocates of the TMT assert that atmospheric and weather conditions make the summit of Maunakea the best possible location for the telescope. But the mountain is also a place that figures centrally in the religious beliefs and ritual life of many native Hawaiians. As the political scientist Iokepa Casumbal-Salazar has explained, a sense of the sacred nature of Maunakea is tied into indigenous accounts of creation. Maunakea was created by the same gods who created the people themselves, making humans and mountain part of a spiritual family. Native Hawaiians have held this peak as sacred land since long before European and American colonization and conquest.

This is land where the god was born, where rituals still take place. Building the TMT, according to the protesters, threatens both that way of life and the spiritual realities that inspire them. Does that make opposition to the telescope 'religious'? As discussed previously, the category of 'religion' is often difficult to separate from other parts of 'culture', especially when looking at areas of the world where those specific and distinct concepts were imposed by colonialism. Native Hawaiian beliefs about the natural world, the gods who created it, and the ongoing relationship between people and the land are in part shaped by descriptions of spiritual realities; but they are also shaped by a long history of political disenfranchisement. In the 19th century, American government and business interests overthrew the independent kingdom of Hawaii, eventually annexing it as a territory and later as a US state. For much of the 20th century, indigenous language and culture was suppressed or denigrated, and assimilation into an English-speaking predominantly Christian lifestyle was rewarded with social advancement. Lands including Maunakea were seized and turned over to government control. By the late 20th century, the state of Hawaii had allowed construction of several telescopes atop Maunakea with little input from indigenous people.

In many ways, the protests at Maunakea resemble indigenous rights movements elsewhere in the USA and across the globe. Since the TMT site was chosen in 2009, protesters have raised concerns about the preservation of their culture and environment, and their inclusion in the political and economic life of the island. They identify the continued construction on Maunakea as assertion of state power over land that was seized from their ancestors. The spiritual or religious meaning of Maunakea to the protesters has always been part of those concerns, but never separated from these other issues. Even as TMT opponents have made use of the law to try to prevent the telescope's construction, they have largely been wary of using a concept of religion that draws a sharp line between religious rights and the cultural, environmental, economic, and political rights that they assert.

Unlike some Christian groups that have fought government seizures of land elsewhere in the United States, TMT protesters have not attempted to argue that their First Amendment constitutional rights to religious freedom are being violated.

Perhaps because the protests in Hawaii are specifically concerned with a telescope, TMT supporters and much of the media coverage beyond Hawaii have been quick to interpret these protests as merely the latest example of a science–religion conflict. Reducing the TMT issue to a story of religion protesting against science made it easier for popular media to describe the protests without acknowledging the nuance of Hawaiian colonial or environmental history or treating it as a local variation on a universal theme. Some commentators equated the concerns of indigenous Hawaiians with religious superstitions, making it possible to dismiss them as unworthy of consideration. A 2014 *New York Times* article argued that TMT protesters were, in effect, 'creationists' indistinguishable from those who held to a literal interpretation of Genesis, but were tolerated 'out of a sense of guilt over past wrongdoings'. This same article even compared the Hawaiian protesters blocking the TMT to the role the Roman Catholic Church played in blocking the dissemination of Galileo's writings. In this conflict narrative, astronomy is always oppressed by religion. A 2015 *Atlantic Magazine* article, however, pointed out that the TMT controversy was more than 'a clash between religion and science'. 'The battle for Mauna Kea', the article argued, 'is ultimately a debate about what is truly sacred, what it means to be human, and who gets to decide.'

In the first chapter, we discussed how it was only through a deliberate and specific process that 'science' and 'religion' became understood as separate categories of knowledge, without which the question of conflict or harmony cannot even make sense. For much of the world outside Europe, that binary way of thinking about science and religion was part of a colonial legacy. In the case of the TMT, it's difficult to distinguish religious elements from other concerns about cultural disregard, political exclusion, environmental degradation, and economic dispossession. A story that imagines marginalized indigenous Hawaiians are the modern equivalents of the 17th-century church, and that a consortium of scientists and universities supported by several of the world's superpowers plays the role of the bullied Galileo, seems preposterous. Nonetheless, the TMT controversy, like the Galileo affair with which we started, shows how debates that seem to be between 'science' and 'religion' tend to conceal struggles for power and control that go beyond those labels.

Like the idea of an inherent science–religion conflict itself, the distorted legacy of Galileo lives on as a convenient mythology in the 21st century. But in the context of Maunakea, these myths are not helping answer questions about the intellectual compatibility of ideas. Instead they are shaping perceptions regarding whose ideas matter at all. Supporters of the TMT can use the framework of science versus religion to argue that opposition to the telescope is 'anti-science' and that concerns about cultural erasure, land seizure, and civil rights are merely 'religious' beliefs that can be dismissed as supernatural. Especially in societies impacted by colonialism and conquest, we see the concepts of science and religion working together like this to establish credibility and authority for certain kinds of knowledge and supplant others.

Medical missions

Perhaps the most visible examples of scientific and religious authority working together in a colonial effort to displace local forms of knowledge is the practice of medicine and knowledge about health. In the 19th century, European nations established hegemony over much of Africa, Asia, and Oceania. In most of these regions, it was not colonial governments but religious societies who assumed the (in their view charitable) task of providing medical care to local populations. For many European Christian organizations, the provision of medical care was often a way to establish credibility and goodwill that could eventually be turned to proselytizing (Figure 12).

As Megan Vaughn has detailed in her history of colonial medicine in Africa, the boundary between secular and religious medicine was often blurry—as Europeans working in medical missions applied knowledge that had itself been developed with particular notions about health, pain, and well-being that were shaped by their own religious world-view. Medical missionaries often combined spiritual messages and prayer with more 'scientific' remedies and frequently interpreted the diseases and conditions they encountered abroad as embodiments of the moral conditions they perceived in the local population. In Africa, European missionaries believed that what they perceived as widespread disease was a consequence of people's non-Christian behaviours. By this they didn't necessarily mean that diseases were a form of divine punishment, but rather that the moral and scientific understanding of the world that (to them) embodied enlightened

12. A Catholic nun working at a health care facility administering Covid-19 vaccinations in Pretoria, South Africa in 2021.

Christianity naturally resulted in better, healthier outcomes. In some cases, this mindset was an extension of natural theological thinking—particularly the notion that correct understanding of God's book of nature provides moral and political guidance that ensures well-being. Just as William Paley diagnosed the human suffering caused by the French Revolution as the moral and political consequences of its rejection of divine order, European medical missionaries sometimes referred to Africa as a 'sick' continent for which the cure was spiritual as well as medical. A small number of medical missionaries, such as Scottish physician and explorer David Livingstone, at least acknowledged the role that centuries of slavery and exploitation had played in creating the 'sickness' of Africa, but from this they inferred that their missionary work was not only an opportunity to save lives and souls. It also represented an act of expiation for the sins of slavery perpetrated by their ancestors.

The experience of Africa as a 'sick' continent by European Christians also illustrates the dynamics of scientific and religious knowledge in colonialism. Missionaries who documented their experiences treating patients inferred that diseases abroad were more prevalent and more dangerous than those in Europe. But if there's credibility to this claim, those conditions can at least partially be ascribed to the spread of diseases from Europe into Africa. In nearly all places where new forms of human colonial contact took place, diseases spread between populations, often to populations with little natural resistance to unfamiliar germs. Infamously, smallpox and other diseases, sometimes deliberately spread by European colonizers, devastated the native peoples of the Americas. European diseases also decimated the island-insulated Hawaiians, weakening their government and economy just as American business interests plotted their coup.

In the case of Africa, not only did colonialism bring new diseases, outbreaks were exacerbated by colonial governments disrupting established local health practices. A few physicians, like Livingstone, attempted to make sense of medical practices he witnessed in Central Africa and understand why they seemed to work. Most, however dismissed out of hand local knowledge that had developed over centuries, especially when healers proffered cures that seemed to rely on supernatural causes. Colonial laws prevented a host of religious healers from practising, and people often had no alternative to missionary medicine, even when it was less effective. The tendency of colonial leaders to view indigenous health practices through the perspective of (good) science and (bad, non-Christian) religion hindered health efforts. In British colonial Kenya, for example, laws against 'witchcraft' made no clear distinctions between a variety of healers and others who performed supernatural works. Colonial categories did not match the way local people understood their own knowledge.

Missionary medical care was frequently supported by church organizations, not as a direct function of the official government. Consequently, religious health organizations sometimes remained in place after colonized regions of Asia and Africa became independent nation-states. In Ghana, the first sub-Saharan African nation to achieve independence, state authorities work with Christian hospitals to advance 'scientific' medicine and to dislodge people's reliance on 'traditional' forms of health practice. Anthropologist Damien Droney has observed that scientific herbal medicine combines modern technology and chemical and biological laboratory analysis with long-used plant-based remedies. This practice establishes scientific credentials that ensure state approval and convince people to use herbal medicine instead of 'magical' alternatives. Part of establishing that this medicine is 'scientific' involves defining scientific herbal medicine as entirely different from the 'religious' identity of 'traditional' medical practices. Droney observes, however, that because of Ghana's history of missionary medicine and education, the concept of 'science' is deeply associated with Christian identity and Ghanaian herbal medicine relies upon church-affiliated hospitals to endorse its claims to be scientific.

Science, religion, and medical knowledge

It is not only the postcolonial world where blurred boundaries between scientific and religious authority affect health and medicine. In 1998, *The Lancet*, one of Britain's most prestigious medical journals, published a study by Andrew Wakefield claiming that the measles, mumps, and rubella (MMR) vaccine caused autism in children. Although the study was eventually determined to be fraudulent and the article was retracted in 2010, the immediate response to Wakefield's study was a decline in vaccination rates in the UK, USA, and elsewhere, followed by outbreaks of once-rare preventable diseases. Although Wakefield's study does not at first seem to invoke any religious views regarding the human body or the efficacy of vaccines, the panic it created found fertile ground in a legal and cultural environment that had been shaped by religious anti-vaccination movements that developed in Europe and North America over centuries.

Vaccinations and inoculations are medical procedures in which a strain of a disease vector (a virus or bacteria, in some cases weakened or killed) is deliberately introduced into a person's body. Typically, this allows the body to develop immunity and reduce the likelihood of becoming sick. Christians in both Europe and North America learned of this practice in the 1700s. In Boston, Massachusetts, the theologian and clergyman Cotton Mather was told about the procedure by Onesimus, an enslaved man brought from West Africa and sold to Mather in 1706. Mather's advocacy of smallpox inoculation was strongly condemned by other clergy in Massachusetts colony, some of whom decried it as going against the will of God. Some of the opposition to Mather also probably stemmed from resentment of his role as the instigator of a series of witch trials in Salem in 1692. Over 200 women and men were tried, and sometimes convicted of gaining supernatural powers from the Devil and using them to harm others. Twenty people were executed, and others died in prison.

News of inoculation first reached Christian parts of Europe in 1717, in letters from Lady Mary Wortley Montagu, wife of the British Ambassador to Constantinople, who witnessed the practice performed by women in the Muslim Ottoman Empire. On both continents, Christian audiences were deeply sceptical of knowledge that came from non-Christian lands, and in both England and the USA the first inoculation trials were primarily attempted upon people who could not consent: condemned prisoners and enslaved Africans, respectively. Attitudes changed after a smallpox outbreak in 1721 devastated Boston, but nearly all of those who had been inoculated survived. One should not imagine that even those who came to accept inoculation in this era understood it as a purely natural phenomenon, nor that it replaced prayer or other healing remedies rather than added to them. It was several years after these trials, after all, that many believed a miracle of St Agatha had saved Catania from the plague.

As these procedures gained credibility, eventually some people went from tolerating vaccinations to requiring them. The US Supreme Court ruled in 1904 that states had the authority to mandate vaccinations, prompting many US states to pass laws creating exemptions on religious grounds. By the late 20th century, these exemptions were little used; however, following the Wakefield fraud, the number of people invoking a religious exemption to vaccination rose dramatically. This does not seem to be because of any major changes in religious attitudes towards vaccines; most major religions not only tolerate but encourage vaccination as part of a moral obligation to preserve life. The rise of religious exemptions speaks instead to a tendency to use legal protections for religious belief as a tool.

Similar circumstances arose in 2020 as the Covid-19 pandemic spread across the globe. Caused by the coronavirus named SARS-CoV-2, the pandemic prompted a range of major public health measures by nearly every nation on Earth. Misinformation about the disease, its effects, and treatments spread almost as rapidly as the virus itself, which affected both how various nations managed the crisis, and how well their population accepted or resisted measures mandated or advised by scientists (Figure 13). In the United States in particular, requirements to close public

13. A sign outside Knox Presbyterian Church in New Westminster, British Columbia encouraging mask wearing during the Covid-19 pandemic in 2020. The sign is a play on the biblical phrase 'Thou shalt not covet'.

venues, including churches, were met with resistance. In May 2020, as cases of Covid-19 continued to increase, several churches in Illinois wrote an open letter threatening to defy the governor's decree prohibiting in-person church gatherings. Some followed through on this threat and were fined. Several other religious groups which defied orders to restrict in-person prayer saw major outbreaks among their communities.

Although some critics claimed that this was yet another example of religious groups refusing to acknowledge scientific fact, most of the churches were less hostile to medical science and more opposed to the government's role in restricting religious practice. In their letter to the governor, the Illinois churches outlined a series of precautions they would take to prevent viral transmission among their members, including the use of sanitizers and social distancing. These congregations were both aware of and accommodating scientific ideas, but they were also asserting the priority of religious freedom over state-mandated health practices.

This is not to say that there were no moments when scientific and religious ideas came into actual conflict during the Covid-19 pandemic. Congregations of Orthodox Christians around the world debated the practice of using a common spoon to partake in communion, with some theologians insisting that because the bread and wine are transubstantiated into the blood and body of Christ, there could be no transmission of the coronavirus through communion. (A similar debate regarding the practice of taking communion from a shared cup took place among some American churches in the early 20th century, as the germ theory of disease became better known. In that case, some denominations split into separate churches over the issue.) More common than these moments of science–religion disagreement, however, were stories of religious communities making use of science and technology to adapt to the pandemic. At Easter, Pope Francis addressed an empty St Peter's Square, and yet his message probably reached a larger audience than any previous one because it was available online. Despite long-standing practices among some Jews not to use electricity on major holidays, several rabbis lifted this prohibition to discourage in-person gatherings and permit virtual Passover Seders and other events to be shared online. And in many parts of the world, religious institutions funded and provided frontline medical services. Many religious organizations also played a key role in ensuring that accurate scientific information reached their communities, helping to limit the spread and deadliness of this plague.

Science 'denial'

In the 21st century, false claims about vaccine safety or misinformation about the treatment and prevention of Covid-19 are among the more dangerous examples of what is often called science 'denial'. This term refers to an organized effort to undermine confidence in well-established scientific knowledge claims, either through casting doubt on scientific evidence or the impartiality of scientists, or by creating seemingly scientific (or pseudoscientific) alternatives to explain the observed world. Anti-evolutionism—particularly versions that promote creation science or intelligent design as 'scientific' alternatives to Darwinian natural selection—is often cited as one of the most widespread and persistent examples of science denial. The idea of the science–religion conflict thesis emerged at a time in the late 19th century when several new religious movements—Jehovah's Witnesses, Christian Scientists, Adventists—all offered as part of their messages claims about science and health that were contrary to prevailing scientific beliefs; and some of the most prominent forms of science denial—such as anti-evolutionism or spiritualism—seemed to be motivated by supernatural ideas or by the perceived threat that scientific ideas presented to religious power and authority.

But increasingly, the motivations for science denial are secular, not religious. Inquiries into the *Lancet* article fraud showed that

Wakefield had hoped to profit from lawsuits against vaccine makers. As historian Robert Proctor has shown, tobacco companies spent years funding studies attempting to refute scientific evidence of a link between smoking and cancer. And protests against scientific recommendations regarding the prevention and treatment of Covid-19 were often fomented along lines of secular political ideology rather than religious belief. Nonetheless, by emphasizing the religiosity of science denial, science advocates portray their opponents as dogmatic and corrupt and themselves as objective and oppressed. Astronomers using a science–religion narrative to dismiss concerns about the TMT on Maunakea is perhaps the most egregious instance of this, considering the balance of political and economic power. As seen in cases regarding quarantine or vaccine refusal, some science deniers embrace a religious identity because by doing so they are able to argue that their views and actions are protected by rights to religious freedom. We began this book by asking: What are science–religion debates really about? Today, they are still less about a substantive debate between particular scientific and religious ideas and more about how the binary thinking they symbolize expresses power and cultural authority.

How it ends

Most of the substantive science and religion issues addressed so far in this book deal with questions of origins (how and when did the Earth and its human inhabitants begin?), morality (how should we act and how can we know whether our ethical beliefs are correct?), or purpose (why are we here and is there anything beyond the natural world itself?). Yet many major religions also address questions of eschatology—how the world ends and what happens to humanity when it does. Almost every religion has traditions or texts that provide predictions and accounts of how things will end, and how humanity's current state of being will culminate. In some Hindu interpretations, a tenth and final incarnation of the god Vishnu will come to the Earth in about

400,000 years, bringing about an end to the current age and leading to a new cycle of birth and growth of the universe. Most Christian traditions believe in a second coming of Jesus, with some interpreting the Book of Revelation to posit times of conflict followed by a final judgement.

Over the past two centuries, scientists have also developed theories about the end of the Earth and the universe. The Sun is a star like many others, and astronomers have detected and described the fate of many similar to our own. Several billion years from now, the Sun will have depleted much of its hydrogen and will expand into a red giant before collapsing into a white dwarf star. Scientists who have studied mass extinctions such as that which killed off the dinosaurs (thought to be the result of an asteroid striking the Earth) consider the possibility of similar catastrophes happening to humanity. In recent years, cosmologists have determined that the expansion of the universe, observed as the movement of galaxies away from one another since the Big Bang, is accelerating. This suggests that one probable outcome for the universe is an ultimate 'heat death' when all mass and energy (or heat) is so thinly spread across the cosmos that no further interactions are possible. There are other potential models for the fate of the cosmological universe many billions of years from now, including the possibility of a 'Big Crunch', a reversal of the expansion that followed the Big Bang. Observations from new, more powerful tools like the TMT may help determine what outcome is most likely.

On questions regarding the end of the world, science and religion may present intellectually incompatible ideas but rarely have been the crux of social conflict. For a long time, scientific eschatology focused on natural processes far beyond the possibility of human intervention. This started to change in the 19th century. One phenomenon that had challenged natural theologians was extinction. For what possible purpose would God create species that would die out, especially in eras long before humanity was present? The question became more complicated as naturalists realized that some species, like the dodo (which had last been observed almost 200 years earlier), had gone extinct due to human activity. Colonists who came to Mauritius in the 17th century cut down much of the dodos' forest habitat and introduced other animals, such as pigs and monkeys, that attacked dodo nests. The religious implications of human-caused extinction were complicated. If each species was distinctly created by God, was permanently destroying a species undoing divine will? Was it inconsistent with the interpretations of the biblical creation story in which God instructed Adam and Eve to have 'dominion' over every living thing on Earth? By the late 19th century, intentional extinction was used as a tool of colonial conquest. US efforts to exterminate the population of American bison were intended to deprive Native Americans of a major food source, legally expropriate their lands (which had been defined in some treaties with reference to their hunting range), and undermine their culture. Lakota consider bison to be sacred animals. By the late 19th century, fewer than 1,000 bison were left alive.

By the 20th century, the reality of long-term and potentially permanent human impacts on the environment were undeniable. In 1962, environmental scientist Rachel Carson published the book *Silent Spring*, whose title evoked the spectre of a world made quiet due to the extinction of wildlife. Carson identified chemical poisoning in the environment as a threat to many species, particularly the agricultural insecticide dichlorodiphenyltrichloroethane (DDT). It had been a century since Darwin had shown how species evolved to fit well with their environment. What happens when that environment drastically changes?

Carson's work inspired a great rise in environmental activism, in the USA and elsewhere. Though *Silent Spring* focuses on the impact of chemicals, it begins by discussing recently discovered effects of radioactive fallout on human beings, another secular apocalyptic threat looming in the midst of the Cold War. However, even before *Silent Spring* reached bookshelves, a concerted effort to cast the book as false had been orchestrated by the American chemical industry that produced DDT and other environmental pollutants. They funded and publicized studies claiming to refute Carson's claim that chemicals lingering in the environment accumulated in animal bodies and disrupted their ability to survive and reproduce. This response was one of the first concerted corporate efforts at science denial. The controversy was mostly secular, but insinuations that Carson was a Communist sympathizer were used to imply that she was an atheist and therefore her morality and loyalty were suspect. Even as US sales of DDT eventually stopped, the chemical industry found profits in much of the tropical postcolonial world, where insecticides were presented as the scientific solution to the scourge of malaria and other insect-transmitted diseases.

The environmental movement that emerged in the 1960s brought together fears of a secular apocalypse caused by new developments in science and technology and long-standing traditions of religious conservationism that had antecedents in natural theology. Historian Mark Stoll traces this history, observing that at various eras in US history, efforts to set aside land as parks and nature reserves were often led by religious individuals for whom nature was a pathway into understanding and appreciating divine creation.

Exemplifying this is the thought of Holmes Rolston III, an American philosopher and theologian whose work helped create academic interest in 'environmental ethics'. Raised in a family of Presbyterian ministers and deeply inspired by natural theology, Rolston attempted to articulate an ethical mandate for environmental stewardship that was not justified by appealing to its direct benefit to humans. Instead, Rolston argued that people, the environment, and non-human nature all have intrinsic value; therefore humanity has obligations to act responsibly and in a caring way for the natural world. In his 1997 Gifford Lectures, Rolston took issue with the evolutionary account of altruism epitomized by Wilson's sociobiology and argued that ethical values—how one goes from describing what behaviour is to what it ought to be—cannot be determined by biology alone. By combining a theological basis for ethics with Wilson's evolutionary insights into the viability of altruism as a moral strategy, Rolston promotes an environmental ethics that not only includes altruism between humans, but also between people and the rest of creation.

According to Rolston, 'Environmental ethics, in this sense, is the most altruistic, global, generous, comprehensive ethic of all, demanding the most expansive capacity to see others, and this now especially distinguishes humans. This is not naturalized ethics in the reductionist sense; it is naturalized ethics in the comprehensive sense, humans acting out of moral conviction for the benefit of nonhuman others.' Rolston and similar thinkers paved the way for some Christian groups that had previously ignored environmental issues, contributing to the rise of lines of thinking sometimes called ecotheology. His work in this field was recognized with the Templeton Prize in 2003.

That Rolston's work was seen as transformative is a result of his efforts to frame such ideas within a new religious and political context, but it also speaks to an intellectual colonialism that took ideas found in other cultural practices and repackaged them as new, whether it's the technique of inoculations or the proposition that people have an ethical duty to the natural world. In this way, the academic field of science and religion uses its proprietary terminology to make new discoveries.

In recent decades, scientists have become increasingly unified in expressing concern about climate change and amassed substantial evidence that human activity—particularly energy consumption associated with increased use of technology—has played a key role in this process. Gases released through fossil fuel burning accumulate in the atmosphere, resulting in more of the Sun's heat trapped on the planet's surface. This can cause prevailing winds and ocean currents to shift, sea ice and frozen land to thaw, and results in both an overall trend of warming and a greater tendency towards more extreme weather events. The planetary climate is a complex, chaotic system, not a reductionistic one, and its patterns are only seen as an emergence from more localized causes and effects. The natural laws that describe it may allow for probabilistic descriptions, but not deterministic accounts of cause and effect.

The complexity of climate science helps explain why climate change denial has been so effective in its message. For decades efforts to take coordinated action to mitigate climate change have been affected by deliberate science denial. There are clear economic and political incentives for this; energy, fuels, and energy technologies play an unparalleled role in global politics. Historians Naomi Oreskes and Eric Conway have found evidence that petrochemical companies deliberately concealed or attempted to cast doubt upon much of the scientific evidence of human-caused climate change, in many cases looking to the history of anti-evolution for strategic inspiration. While most forms of climate change denial do not explicitly invoke religion or theology, some of the rhetoric invoked echoes of themes introduced in earlier debates over extinction. If this is the world that God has made, can any human force be so great as to undo it?

With the harmful effects of climate change becoming more visible to a larger population, it will increasingly loom as the great challenge that science and religion will need to speak to in the decades to come. Although much of the well-funded sophisticated efforts to spread climate change denial are secular in both origin and rhetoric, it's not unusual to hear claims that human impacts cannot possibly undo the whole of creation, or that the effects of climate change are part of a period of tribulation that precedes divine redemption. But growing louder are religious voices who speak to an ethical responsibility to care for creation. The effects of climate change and other forms of environmental damage often weigh most heavily on the postcolonial world and on impoverished and marginalized people in every country. Yet it is the countries that historically have been colonial powers that have been responsible for consuming the majority of the fossil fuels and producing industrial pollutants that have led to environmental degradation. Finding a just reconciliation of this history requires more than simply a technological solution. As the climate crisis contributes to lands lost to sea rise, droughts, and extreme storms, this is likely to result in people migrating from ancestral lands, and, as Malthus hypothesized, conflict over scarce resources.

It is important to recognize the influence of thinkers like Rolston while also acknowledging that an ethical mandate for environmental care and belief in common kinship between humanity and non-human elements of nature is a long-standing feature of other religions and cultures. It is present in Hindu and Buddhist beliefs that souls reincarnate, and that a human soul may be reborn to a new life as a different species. It is present in the belief of Native Hawaiians that they were created as part of the same family as the mountain Maunakea.

Answering questions about what steps represent a path forward will rely on finding a synthesis of scientific and technological possibilities with insights into justice and ethics that religion can provide. Looking to the future, there is every reason to believe that ideas about science and religion will continue to shape those discussions. It is to be hoped that with greater awareness of what science and religion are, what their historical relationship has been, and who has controlled the dialogue between them, more fruitful interactions will follow.

References

Abbreviations for websites cited more than once:

CCEL   Christian Classics Ethereal Library: <http://www.ccel.org/>

CWCD   The Complete Works of Charles Darwin Online: <http://darwin-online.org.uk/>

FT   Famous Trials website: <https://famous-trials.com/>

PG   Project Gutenberg: <http://www.gutenberg.org/>

TP   Thomas Paine National Historical Association: <http://www.thomaspaine.org/>

This list gives references for material directly quoted in the text. The Further reading section gives suggested background reading and additional sources.

Where reputable online editions of works are available, these have been cited in addition to the original published source. Different English translations of biblical passages can be compared online at The Bible Gateway: <http://www.biblegateway.com/>

Chapter 1: What are science–religion debates really about?

Galileo's condemnation: Mario Biagioli, *Galileo, Courtier: The Practice of Science in the Culture of Absolutism* (Chicago, 1994), quotation at pp. 330–1. Documents relating to Galileo's trial and condemnation can be found online at FT. Psalm 102:25. Thomas Huxley's review of *The Origin of Species* was originally published in

1860 in the *Westminster Review* and was reprinted in Volume 2 of his *Collected Essays* (9 volumes, London, 1893-4), pp. 22-79, quotation at p. 52; available online at The Huxley File at Clark University: <http://aleph0.clarku.edu/huxley/>. John Hedley Brooke, *Science and Religion: Some Historical Perspectives* (Cambridge, 1991), quotation at p. 5.

Quotation from Galileo Galilei, *Dialogue Concerning the Two Chief World Systems* (1632), in William Shea, 'Galileo's Copernicanism: The Science and the Rhetoric', in *The Cambridge Companion to Galileo*, ed. Peter Machamer (Cambridge, 1998), pp. 211-43, quotation at p. 238. Psalm 19:1. Thomas Paine, *The Age of Reason, Part I* (1794), in *Thomas Paine: Political Writings*, ed. Bruce Kuklick (Cambridge, 1989), quotations from chapters 7, 11, and 16; available online at TP.

Chapter 2: Galileo and the philosophy of science

Documents relating to Galileo's trial and condemnation can be found at FT. Francis Bacon, *The New Organon, or True Directions Concerning the Interpretation of Nature* (1620), Aphorism III; *Valerius Terminus: Of the Interpretation of Nature* (1603), chapter 1. Both these works are available in modern editions, and also online at the University of Adelaide: <http://etext.library. adelaide.edu.au/>. Thomas Paine, *The Age of Reason, Part I* (1794), in *Thomas Paine: Political Writings*, ed. Bruce Kuklick (Cambridge, 1989), chapter 2; available online at TP. Joshua 10:12-14. Council of Trent declaration: Richard Blackwell, 'Could There Be Another Galileo Case?', in *The Cambridge Companion to Galileo*, ed. Peter Machamer (Cambridge, 1998), pp. 348-66, quotation at p. 353. Romans 1:20.

Chapter 3: God and nature

Milk miracle: 'Right-Wing Hindus Milk India's "Miracle"', *The Independent* (London), 25 September 1995, p. 11. Olive oil: 'A Virgin Mary Statue has been "Weeping" Olive Oil. Church Leaders Can't Explain it', *The Washington Post*, 18 July 2018. Friedrich Schleiermacher, *On Religion: Speeches to its Cultured Despisers*, ed. Richard Crouter (Cambridge, 1996), Second Speech, quotation at p. 49; first published in German in 1799; available online at CCEL. Henry Drummond, *The Lowell Lectures on the Ascent of*

Man (1894), chapter 10; available online at CCEL. G. W. Leibniz, 'Mr Leibnitz's First Paper', in Samuel Clarke, *A Collection of Papers, Which passed between the late Learned Mr. Leibnitz, and Dr. Clarke, In the Years 1715 and 1716* (1717); available online at The Newton Project at Sussex University: <http://www.newtonproject. sussex.ac.uk/>. Laplace and Napoleon: Roger Hahn, 'Laplace and the Mechanistic Universe', in *God and Nature: Historical Essays on the Encounter between Christianity and Science*, ed. David C. Lindberg and Ronald L. Numbers (Berkeley, 1986), pp. 256–76, quotation at p. 256. Descartes to Mersenne: quoted in Carolyn Merchant, *The Death of Nature: Women, Ecology, and the Scientific Revolution* (San Francisco, 1983), p. 205. Nancy Cartwright uses the phrase 'dappled world' to echo Gerard Manley Hopkins's poem 'Pied Beauty', which starts with the line 'Glory be to God for dappled things'; Nancy Cartwright, *The Dappled World: A Study of the Boundaries of Science* (Cambridge, 1999), Part I, quotation from Hopkins at p. 19. Einstein made comments about God not playing dice on several occasions, including in a letter to the physicist Max Born in 1926; Abraham Pais, *Subtle is the Lord: The Science and the Life of Albert Einstein*, new edition (Oxford, 2005), chapter 25. Pius XII, 'The Proofs for the Existence of God in the Light of Modern Natural Science', address delivered 22 November 1951, published in English as 'Theology and Modern Science', *The Tablet* (1 December 1951), p. 392. Francis Bacon, *The Advancement of Learning*, Book II (1605). Steven Shapin and Simon Shaffer, *Leviathan and the Air Pump: Hobbes, Boyle, and the Experimental* Life (Princeton, 1985). J. Topham, 'Science and Popular Education in the 1830s: The Role of the Bridgewater Treatises', *The British Journal for the History of Science*, vol. 25, issue 4 (1992), pp. 397–430 doi:10.1017/S0007087400029587. David Hume, *Dialogues Concerning Natural Religion* (1779), Part II; available in several modern editions, and online at PG. Thomas Malthus, *An Essay on the Principle of Population* (London, 1798), chapter 18; available on PG.

Chapter 4: Darwin and evolution

Charles Lyell used the phrase 'go the whole orang' in a letter to Darwin in March 1863. Frederick Burkhardt and Sydney Smith (eds), *The Correspondence of Charles Darwin, Volume 11: 1863* (Cambridge, 1985), pp. 230–3; this letter is available online at The Darwin

Correspondence Project: <http://www.darwinproject.ac.uk/>. Quotations from Darwin's *Beagle* notebooks: Adrian Desmond and James Moore, *Darwin* (London, 1991), pp. 122, 176. Darwin's comments on the 'damnable doctrine' of damnation, and on preferring the label 'agnostic', are made in the section of his autobiography concerning religious belief, *The Autobiography of Charles Darwin*, ed. Nora Barlow (London, 1958), pp. 85–96, quotations at pp. 87, 94; available online at CWCD. *The Origin of Species by Means of Natural Selection* (1859) is available in many modern editions, and online at CWCD, where changes between editions can also be compared, such as the insertion of 'by the Creator' at the end of the 1860 second edition, at p. 490. On Darwin's attitudes towards Paley, *The Autobiography of Charles Darwin*, p. 87. Charles Kingsley, *The Water Babies* (1863), chapter 7, p. 315; available online at PG. Samuel Wilberforce's review of *The Origin of Species* in the *Quarterly Review* 108 (1860), pp. 225–64, quotations at pp. 231, 259–60; available online at CWCD. Huxley's and others' recollections of the 1860 Oxford debate are discussed in Frank James, 'An "Open Clash between Science and the Church"? Wilberforce, Huxley and Hooker on Darwin at the British Association, Oxford, 1860', in *Science and Beliefs: From Natural Philosophy to Natural Science, 1700–1900*, ed. D. Knight and M. Eddy (Aldershot, 2005), pp. 171–93, quotation from Huxley at p. 185. See also Leonard Huxley, *The Life and Letters of Thomas Henry Huxley*, 2 vols (London, 1900); selections available online through the '20th Century Commentary' section of HF. Tennessee's 1925 anti-evolution statute is quoted in Edward J. Larson, *Summer for the Gods: The Scopes Trial and America's Continuing Debate over Science and Religion* (Cambridge, Mass., 1997), p. 50. The text of the statute is available online at FT. Bryan's comments on 'the little circle entitled "Mammals"' come from the speech he intended to deliver to the jury as the closing argument for the prosecution in the Scopes trial. Darrow's decision to submit the case to the jury without argument prevented Bryan from delivering the speech, which is included as an appendix to William Jennings Bryan and Mary Baird Bryan, *The Memoirs of William Jennings Bryan* (Philadelphia, 1925), quotation at p. 535. Genesis 1:26. Extracts from the transcript of the Scopes trial, including the cross-examination of Bryan by Darrow, are available online at FT. Text of Arkansas 'Balanced Treatment' law quoted in the court ruling *McLean v. Arkansas*

Board of Education (1982) included as an appendix to Langdon
Gilkey, *Creationism on Trial: Evolution and God at Little Rock*
(Charlottesville, Va., 1998), quotation at p. 295. The full text of
Judge John E. Jones III's ruling in the Dover case in 2005 is
available on the NCSE website: <https://ncse.ngo/files/pub/legal/
kitzmiller/highlights/2005-12-20>_Kitzmiller_decision.pdf>.
Peter Gottschalk, *Religion, Science, and Empire: Classifying
Hinduism and Islam in British India* (Oxford 2013), quotation
on p. 44. On Havasupai: Robyn L. Sterling, 'Genetic Research
Among the Havasupai: A Cautionary Tale', *American Medical
Association Journal of Ethics* (February 2011), pp. 113–17. Kim
TallBear, 'Tell Me a Story: Genomics vs. Indigenous Origin
Narratives', *GeneWatch* (August–October 2013).

Chapter 5: Mind, brain, and morality

Mario Beauregard and Vincent Paquette, 'Neural Correlates of a
Mystical Experience in Carmelite Nuns', *Neuroscience Letters*,
vol. 405, issue 3 (25 September 2006), pp. 186–90; reported in *The
Daily Telegraph* (London), 30 August 2006, p. 12, as 'Nuns Prove
God Is Not Figment of the Mind'; available online via <http://
www.telegraph.co.uk/>. 'Let us eat and drink for tomorrow we die'
is a biblical phrase: 1 Corinthians 15:32; see also Ecclesiastes 8:15,
Isaiah 22:13, Luke 12:19–20. Francis Collins on altruism: *The
Language of God: A Scientist Presents Evidence for Belief* (New
York, 2006), pp. 21–31. Biology, politics, and race: Dorothy
Roberts, *Fatal Invention: How Science, Politics, and Big Business
Re-create Race in the 21st Century* (New York, 2011). On situated
knowledge: Donna Haraway, 'Situated Knowledges: The Science
Question in Feminism and the Privilege of Partial Perspective',
Feminist Studies, vol. 14, no. 3 (Autumn 1988), pp. 575–99.

Chapter 6: The worlds of science and religion

On TMT and protests: Iokepa Casumbal-Salazar, 'A Fictive Kinship:
Making "Modernity," "Ancient Hawaiians," and the Telescopes on
Mauna Kea', *Native American and Indigenous Studies* (2017).
Korey Haynes, 'Protests Resume in Hawaii with Start of Thirty
Meter Telescope Construction', *Discover*, 16 July 2019; available
online via <http://www.discovermagazine.com>. George Johnson,
'Seeking Stars, Finding Creationism', *The New York Times*, 20

October 2014; available online via <http://www.nytimes.com>. Adrienne LaFrance, 'The Thirty Meter Telescope and the Fight for Hawaii's Future', *The Atlantic*, 30 October 2015; available online via <http://www.theatlantic.com>. On colonial medicine: Megan Vaughn, *Curing Their Ills: Colonial Power and African Illness* (Cambridge, 1991). C. Clifton Roberts, 'Witchcraft and Colonial Legislation', *Africa: Journal of the International African Institute* (October 1935). Damien Droney, *Weedy Science: Projects of Herbal Medicine in Postcolonial Ghana* (forthcoming). Jennifer Lee Carrell, *The Speckled Monster: A Historical Tale of Battling Smallpox* (New York, 2003). Adam Shapiro, 'Are Pandemic Protests the Newest Form of Science-Religion Conflict?', *Religion & Politics*, 14 July 2020; available online via <http://www.religionandpolitics.org>. Robert N. Proctor, *Cancer Wars: How Politics Shapes What We Know and Don't Know about Cancer* (New York, 1995). Mark V. Barrow, *Nature's Ghosts: Confronting Extinction from the Age of Jefferson to the Age of Ecology* (Chicago, 2009). Rachel Carson, *Silent Spring* (New York, 1962). Mark R. Stoll, *Inherit the Holy Mountain: Religion and the Ride of American Environmentalism* (Oxford, 2015). Holmes Rolston III, *Genes, Genesis and God: Values and their Origins in Natural and Human History* (Cambridge, 1999); quotation on page 288. Naomi Oreskes and Erik M. Conway, *Merchants of Doubt: How a Handful of Scientists Obscured the Truth on Issues from Tobacco Smoke to Global Warming* (New York, 2010).

Further reading

General

Reference works

Philip Clayton and Zachary Simpson (eds), *The Oxford Handbook of Religion and Science* (Oxford and New York, 2006).

Gary B. Ferngren (ed.), *The History of Science and Religion in the Western Tradition: An Encyclopedia* (New York and London, 2000).

J. Wentzel van Huyssteen (ed.), *Encyclopedia of Science and Religion*, 2 vols (New York, 2003).

Historical studies

John Hedley Brooke, *Science and Religion: Some Historical Perspectives* (Cambridge, 1991).

John Brooke and Geoffrey Cantor, *Reconstructing Nature: The Engagement of Science and Religion* (Edinburgh, 1998).

Peter Harrison, *The Territories of Science and Religion* (Chicago, 2015).

David Knight and Matthew Eddy (eds), *Science and Beliefs: From Natural Philosophy to Natural Science* (Aldershot, 2005).

Bernard Lightman (ed.), *Rethinking History, Science, and Religion: An Exploration of Conflict and the Complexity Principle* (Pittsburgh, 2019).

David C. Lindberg and Ronald L. Numbers (eds), *God and Nature: Historical Essays on the Encounter between Christianity and Science* (Berkeley, 1986), and *When Science and Christianity Meet* (Chicago and London, 2003).

Overviews from Christian perspectives

Ian Barbour, *Religion and Science: Historical and Contemporary Issues* (San Francisco, 1997).

Alister E. McGrath, *Science and Religion: An Introduction* (Oxford, 1998).

Arthur Peacocke, *Creation and the World of Science: The Reshaping of Belief*, revised edition (Oxford and New York, 2004).

John Polkinghorne, *Theology and Science: An Introduction* (London, 1998).

Islamic science

Taner Edis, *An Illusion of Harmony: Science and Religion in Islam* (Amherst, NY, 2007).

Muzaffar Iqbal, *Islam and Science* (Aldershot, 2002), and *Science and Islam* (Westport, Conn., 2007).

Seyyed Hossein Nasr, *Science and Civilisation in Islam*, 2nd edition (Cambridge, 1987).

George Saliba, *Islamic Science and the Making of the European Renaissance* (Cambridge, Mass., 2007).

M. Alper Yalçinkaya, *Learned Patriots: Debating Science, State and Society in the Nineteenth-Century Ottoman Empire* (Chicago, 2015).

Judaism and science

Geoffrey Cantor, *Quakers, Jews, and Science: Religious Responses to Modernity and the Sciences in Britain, 1650–1900* (Oxford and New York, 2005).

Noah J. Efron, *Judaism and Science: A Historical Introduction* (Westport, Conn., 2007).

Jonathan Sacks, *The Great Partnership: Science, Religion, and the Search for Meaning* (New York, 2011).

Hinduism and science

Cheever Mackenzie Brown, *Hindu Perspectives on Evolution: Darwin, Dharma, and Design* (London, 2012).

Global perspectives

John Hedley Brooke and Ronald L. Numbers (eds), *Science and Religion Around the World* (Oxford, 2011).

Catherine Keller and Mary-Jane Rubenstein (eds), *Entangled Worlds: Religion, Science, and New Materialisms* (New York, 2017).

Fraser Watts and Kevin Dutton (eds), *Why the Science and Religion Dialogue Matters: Voices from the International Society for Science and Religion* (Philadelphia and London, 2006).

Websites

American Association for the Advancement of Science Dialog on Science, Ethics and Religion: <http://www.aaas.org/programs/dialogue-science-ethics-and-religion

Center for Islam and Science: http://www.cis-ca.org/>

Center for Theology and the Natural Sciences: <http://www.ctns.org/>

International Society for Science and Religion: <http://www.issr.org.uk/?>

John Templeton Foundation: <http://www.templeton.org/>

National Center for Science Education: <http://www.ncse.org/>

Stanford Encyclopedia of Philosophy: <http://plato.stanford.edu/?>

TalkOrigins Archive: Exploring the Evolution/Creation Controversy: <http://www.talkorigins.org/?>

Chapter 1: What are science–religion debates really about?

Religious belief and the birth of modern science

Peter Dear, *Revolutionizing the Sciences: European Knowledge and its Ambitions, 1500–1700* (Basingstoke, 2001).

Peter Harrison, *The Bible, Protestantism, and the Rise of Natural Science* (Cambridge, 2008).

Steven Shapin, *The Scientific Revolution* (Chicago, 1996).

Books by religious scientists

Francis Collins, *The Language of God: A Scientist Presents Evidence for Belief* (New York, 2006).

Guy Consolmagno, *God's Mechanics: How Scientists and Engineers Make Sense of Religion* (San Francisco, 2007).

Owen Gingerich, *God's Universe* (Cambridge, Mass., 2006).

John Polkinghorne, *Belief in God in an Age of Science* (New Haven, 1998).

Thomas Paine

Thomas Paine, *Political Writings*, ed. Bruce Kuklick (Cambridge, 1989); Paine's major works are available online at TP.

Gregory Claeys, *Thomas Paine: Social and Political Thought* (Boston and London, 1989).

John Keane, *Tom Paine: A Political Life* (London, 1996).

Leigh Eric Schmidt, *The Church of Saint Thomas Paine: A Religious History of American Secularism* (Princeton, 2021).

Science and atheism

Elaine Howard Ecklund and David R. Johnson, *Varieties of Atheism in Science* (Oxford, 2021).

Nathan Johnstone, *The New Atheism, Myth, and History. The Black Legends of Contemporary Anti-Religion* (London, 2018).

Shoaib Ahmed Malik, *Atheism and Islam: A Contemporary Discourse* (Abu Dhabi, 2018).

Victor J. Stenger, *God: The Failed Hypothesis. How Science Shows that God Does Not Exist* (Amherst, 2007).

Natural theology

John Hedley Brooke, *Science and Religion: Some Historical Perspectives* (Cambridge, 1991).

Russell Re Manning (ed.), *The Oxford Handbook of Natural Theology* (Oxford, 2013).

Chapter 2: Galileo and the philosophy of science

Philosophy of science

A. F. Chalmers, *What Is This Thing Called Science?*, 3rd edition (Buckingham, 1999).

Peter Godfrey-Smith, *Theory and Reality: An Introduction to the Philosophy of Science* (Chicago, 2003).

Samir Okasha, *Philosophy of Science: A Very Short Introduction* (Oxford, 2002).

Philosophy of science in theological perspective

Philip Clayton, *Explanation from Physics to Theology: An Essay in Rationality and Religion* (New Haven, 1989).

Christopher Knight, *Wrestling with the Divine: Religion, Science, and Revelation* (Minneapolis, 2001).

Galileo and the Church

John Brooke and Geoffrey Cantor, *Reconstructing Nature: The Engagement of Science and Religion* (Edinburgh, 1998).

J. L. Heilbron, *The Sun in the Church: Cathedrals as Solar Observatories* (Cambridge, Mass., 1999).

Peter Machamer (ed.), *The Cambridge Companion to Galileo* (Cambridge, 1998).

Ernan McMullin (ed.), *The Church and Galileo* (Notre Dame, Ind., 2005).

Realism, philosophy, and science

Ian Hacking, *Representing and Intervening* (Cambridge, 1983).

Thomas Kuhn, *The Structure of Scientific Revolutions*, 3rd edition (Chicago and London, 1996); first published 1962.

Peter Lipton, *Inference to the Best Explanation*, 2nd edition (London, 2004).

Richard Rorty, *Philosophy and Social Hope* (London, 1999).

Bas van Fraassen, *The Scientific Image* (Oxford, 1980).

Realism and theology

Colin Crowder (ed.), *God and Reality: Essays on Christian Non-Realism* (London, 1997).

Don Cupitt, *Taking Leave of God* (London, 1980).

Michael Scott and Andrew Moore (eds), *Realism and Religion: Philosophical and Theological Perspectives* (Aldershot, 2007).

Janet Soskice, *Metaphor and Religious Language* (Oxford, 1985).

Chapter 3: God and nature

Miracles

David Corner, *The Philosophy of Miracles* (London, 2007).

John Earman, *Hume's Abject Failure: The Argument Against Miracles* (New York, 2000).

Robert J. Fogelin, *A Defense of Hume on Miracles* (Princeton, 2003).

Robert B. Mullin, *Miracles and the Modern Religious Imagination* (New Haven and London, 1996).

Jane Shaw, *Miracles in Enlightenment England* (New Haven and London, 2006).

God and physics

Philip Clayton, *God and Contemporary Science* (Edinburgh, 1997).

Paul Davies, *The Mind of God: Science and the Search for Ultimate Meaning* (London, 1992).

Willem B. Drees, *Beyond the Big Bang: Quantum Cosmologies and God* (La Salle, Ill., 1990).

John Polkinghorne, *The Faith of a Physicist* (Princeton, 1994), also published as *Science and Christian Belief* (London, 1994).

Nicholas Saunders, *Divine Action and Modern Science* (Cambridge, 2002).

Laws of nature

Nancy Cartwright, *How the Laws of Physics Lie* (Oxford, 1983), and
   The Dappled World: A Study of the Boundaries of Science
   (Cambridge, 1999).
John Dupré, *The Disorder of Things: Metaphysical Foundations of the
   Disunity of Science* (Cambridge, Mass., 1993).
Bas van Fraassen, *Laws and Symmetry* (Oxford, 1989).
Ursula Goodenough, *The Sacred Depths of Nature* (Oxford, 1998).

Quantum physics

Karen Barad, *Meeting the Universe Halfway: Quantum Physics and
   the Entanglement of Matter and Meaning* (Durham, 2007).
George Johnson, *Fire in the Mind: Science, Faith, and the Search for
   Order* (New York, 1995).
John Polkinghorne, *Quantum Theory: A Very Short Introduction*
   (Oxford, 2002), and *Quantum Physics and Theology: An
   Unexpected Kinship* (London, 2007).

Chapter 4: Darwin and evolution

Charles Darwin

Janet Browne, *Darwin: A Biography*, 2 vols (London, 1995, 2002).
Charles Darwin, *The Autobiography of Charles Darwin*, ed. Nora
   Barlow (London, 1958), available online at CWCD.
Adrian Desmond, James Moore, and Janet Browne, *Charles Darwin*
   (Oxford, 2007).
Jonathan Hodge and Gregory Radick (eds), *The Cambridge
   Companion to Darwin* (Cambridge, 2003).

History of biology

Peter J. Bowler, *Evolution: The History of an Idea*, 3rd edition (Berkeley
   and London, 2003), and *The Eclipse of Darwinism: Anti-Darwinian
   Evolution Theories in the Decades around 1900* (Baltimore, 1992).
Jim Endersby, *A Guinea Pig's History of Biology: The Plants and
   Animals Who Taught Us the Facts of Life* (London, 2007).

Darwinism and religion

Peter J. Bowler, *Monkey Trials and Gorilla Sermons: Evolution and
   Christianity from Darwin to Intelligent Design* (Cambridge, Mass.,
   and London, 2007).

C. Mackenzie Brown (ed.), *Asian Religious Responses to Darwinism* (Cham, 2020).

Marwa Elshakry, *Reading Darwin in Arabic* (Chicago, 2013).

David N. Livingstone, *Dealing with Darwin: Place, Politics, and Rhetoric in Religious Engagements with Evolution* (Baltimore, 2014).

James Moore, *The Post-Darwinian Controversies: A Study of the Protestant Struggle to Come to Terms with Darwin in Great Britain and America, 1870–1900* (Cambridge, 1979), and *The Darwin Legend* (Grand Rapids, Mich., 1994).

Michael Ruse, *Darwin and Design: Does Evolution Have a Purpose?* (Cambridge, Mass., 2003).

Thomas Huxley and Victorian science

Adrian Desmond, *Huxley: From Devil's Disciple to Evolution's High Priest* (London, 1998).

Bernard Lightman (ed.), *Victorian Science in Context* (Chicago, 1997).

Frank M. Turner, *Contesting Cultural Authority: Essays in Victorian Intellectual Life* (Cambridge, 1993).

Paul White, *Thomas Huxley: Making the 'Man of Science'* (Cambridge, 2003).

Theology and evolution

Geoffrey Cantor and Marc Swelitz (eds), *Jewish Tradition and the Challenge of Darwinism* (Chicago, 2006).

Johan De Smedt and Helen De Cruz, *The Challenge of Evolution to Religion* (Cambridge, 2020).

John F. Haught, *God After Darwin: A Theology of Evolution* (Boulder, Colo., and Oxford, 2000).

Nancey Murphy and William R. Stoeger, SJ (eds), *Evolution and Emergence: Systems, Organisms, Persons* (Oxford, 2007).

Arthur Peacocke, *Theology for a Scientific Age: Being and Becoming—Natural, Divine, and Human*, enlarged edition (Minneapolis and London, 1993).

Michael Ruse, *Can a Darwinian Be a Christian? The Relationship between Science and Religion* (Cambridge and New York, 2001).

Creationism

Dorothy Nelkin, *The Creation Controversy: Science or Scripture in the Schools?* (New York, 1982).

Ronald L. Numbers, *The Creationists: From Scientific Creationism to Intelligent Design*, expanded edition (Cambridge, Mass., and London, 2006).

Eugenie C. Scott, *Evolution versus Creationism: An Introduction* (Westport, Conn., 2004).

The Scopes trial

Edward J. Larson, *Summer for the Gods: The Scopes Trial and America's Continuing Debate over Science and Religion* (New York, 1997).

Adam R. Shapiro, *Trying Biology: The Scopes Trial, Textbooks, and the Antievolution Movement in American Schools* (Chicago, 2013).

Legal aspects

Langdon Gilkey, *Creationism on Trial: Evolution and God at Little Rock* (Charlottesville, Va., 1998).

Marcel La Follette (ed.), *Creationism, Science, and the Law: The Arkansas Case* (Cambridge, Mass., 1983).

Edward J. Larson, *Trial and Error: The American Controversy over Creation and Evolution*, 3rd edition (New York and Oxford, 2003).

Nicholas J. Matzke, 'The Evolution of Antievolution Policies after Kitzmiller v. Dover', *Science*, vol. 351, 6268 (1 January 2016), pp. 28–30.

Intelligent design

Michael J. Behe, *Darwin's Black Box: The Biochemical Challenge to Evolution* (New York, 1996), and *The Edge of Evolution: The Search for the Limits of Darwinism* (New York, 2007).

William Dembski and Michael Ruse (eds), *Debating Design: From Darwin to DNA* (Cambridge, 2004).

Kenneth R. Miller, *Finding Darwin's God: A Scientist's Search for Common Ground between God and Evolution* (New York, 1999).

Robert T. Pennock (ed.), *Intelligent Design Creationism and its Critics: Philosophical, Theological, and Scientific Perspectives* (Cambridge, Mass., 2001).

Chapter 5: Mind, brain, and morality

Brain and mind

Antonio Damasio, *Descartes' Error: Emotion, Reason, and the Human Brain*, revised edition (London, 2006).

John Searle, *Mind: A Brief Introduction* (Oxford, 2004).

Neuroscience, psychology, and religion

C. Daniel Batson, Patricia Schoenrade, and W. Larry Ventis, *Religion and the Individual: A Social-Psychological Perspective* (New York and Oxford, 1993).

Warren S. Brown, Nancey Murphy, and H. Newton Malony, *Whatever Happened to the Soul? Scientific and Theological Portraits of Human Nature* (Minneapolis, 1998).

John Lardas Modern, *Neuromatic Or, A Particular History of Religion and the Brain* (Chicago, 2021).

Nancey Murphy and Warren S. Brown, *Did My Neurons Make Me Do It? Philosophical and Neurobiological Perspectives on Moral Responsibility and Free Will* (Oxford, 2007).

Andrew Newberg, Eugene d'Aquili, and Vince Rause, *Why God Won't Go Away: Brain Science and the Biology of Belief* (New York, 2002).

Fraser Watts, *Theology and Psychology* (Aldershot, 2002).

Cognitive science and anthropology of religion

Scott Atran, *In Gods We Trust: The Evolutionary Landscape of Religion* (London and New York, 2002).

Pascal Boyer, *Religion Explained: The Human Instincts that Fashion Gods, Spirits and Ancestors* (London, 2001).

Steven Mithen, *The Prehistory of the Mind: The Search for the Origins of Art, Religion and Science* (London, 1996).

Wentzel van Huyssteen, *Alone in the World? Human Uniqueness in Science and Theology: The Gifford Lectures* (Grand Rapids, Mich., 2006).

Evolution and ethics

Stephen R. L. Clark, *Biology and Christian Ethics* (Cambridge, 2000).

Daniel C. Dennett, *Darwin's Dangerous Idea: Evolution and the Meanings of Life* (London and New York, 1995).

Frans de Waal, *Primates and Philosophers: How Morality Evolved* (Princeton and Oxford, 2006).

Thomas Huxley, *Evolution and Ethics, and Other Essays*, in *Collected Essays* (London, 1893–4), vol. 9; available online at HF.

Mary Midgley, *Beast and Man: The Roots of Human Nature*, new edition (London and New York, 1995).

Altruism and selfishness

Richard Dawkins, *The Selfish Gene* (New York and Oxford, 1976).

Thomas Dixon, *The Invention of Altruism: Making Moral Meanings in Victorian Britain* (Oxford, 2008).

Stephen G. Post, Lynn G. Underwood, Jeffrey P. Schloss, and William B. Hurlbut (eds), *Altruism and Altruistic Love: Science, Philosophy and Religion in Dialogue* (Oxford and New York, 2002).

David Sloan Wilson, *Does Altruism Exist? Culture, Genes, and the Welfare of Others* (New Haven, 2015).

Gender, sexuality, and society

Austen Hartke, *Transforming: The Bible and the Lives of Transgender Christians* (Louisville, Ky., 2018).

Roy Porter and Lesley Hall, *The Facts of Life: The Creation of Sexual Knowledge in Britain, 1650–1950* (New Haven, 1995).

Kathleen M. Sands (ed.), *God Forbid: Religion and Sex in American Public Life* (Oxford, 2000).

Jeffrey Weeks, *Sex, Politics and Society: The Regulation of Sexuality since 1800*, 2nd edition (London, 1989), and *Coming Out: Homosexual Politics in Britain from the Nineteenth Century to the Present*, revised edition (London, 1990).

The naturalistic fallacy

Alasdair MacIntyre, *After Virtue: A Study in Moral Theory*, 2nd edition (Notre Dame, Ind., 1984).

G. E. Moore, *Principia ethica*, edited with an introduction by Thomas Baldwin (Cambridge, 1993); first published 1903.

Feminist epistemology of science

Donna Haraway, *Simians, Cyborgs, and Women* (New York, 1991).

Sandra Harding, *Whose Science? Whose Knowledge?* (Ithaca, NY, 1991).

Evelyn Fox Keller, *Reflections on Gender and Science* (New Haven, 1985).

Helen E. Longino, *Science as Social Knowledge* (Princeton, 1990).

Londa Schiebinger *The Mind Has No Sex?* (Cambridge, Mass., 1989).

Science and the future

Stephen R. L. Clark, *How to Live Forever: Science Fiction and Philosophy* (London and New York, 1995).

Mary Midgley, *Science as Salvation: A Modern Myth and its Meaning* (London and New York, 1992), and *Evolution as a Religion: Strange Hopes and Stranger Fears*, revised edition (London and New York, 2002).

John Polkinghorne and Michael Welker (eds), *The End of the World and the Ends of God: Science and Theology on Eschatology* (Harrisburg, 2000).

Chapter 6: The worlds of science and religion

Hawaii/Thirty Meter Telescope

Noelani Goodyear-Kaopua, Ikaika Hussey, and Erin Kahunawaika 'ala Wright (eds), *A Nation Rising: Hawaiian Movements for Life, Land, and Sovereignty* (Durham, NC, 2014).

Chanda Prescod-Weinstein, *The Disordered Cosmos: A Journey into Dark Matter, Spacetime, & Dreams Deferred* (New York, 2021).

Michael J. West, *A Sky Wonderful with Stars: 50 Years of Modern Astronomy on Maunakea* (Honolulu, 2015).

Colonial medicine and bioscience

Hartford Institute for Religion Research, *Navigating the Pandemic: A First Look at Congregational Responses* (Hartford, Conn., 2021).

Suman Seth, *Difference and Disease: Race and the Eighteenth-Century British Empire* (Cambridge, 2018).

Kim TallBear, *Native American DNA: Tribal Belonging and the False Promise of Genetic Science* (Minneapolis, 2013).

Helen C. Tilley, *Africa as a Living Laboratory: Empire, Development, and the Problem of Scientific Knowledge* (Chicago, 2011).

Environmentalism and religion

Celia E. Deane-Drummond, *The Ethics of Nature* (Malden, Mass., 2004).

Katherine Hayhoe, *Saving Us: A Climate Scientist's Case for Hope and Healing in a Divided World* (New York, 2021).

Bron Taylor (ed.), *Encyclopedia of Religion and Nature* (London, 2005).

Science denial

Michael Gordin, *The Pseudoscience Wars: Immanuel Velikovsky and the Birth of the Modern Fringe* (Chicago, 2013).

Naomi Oreskes, *Why Trust Science?* (Princeton, 2019).

Index

For the benefit of digital users, indexed terms that span two pages (e.g., 52–53) may, on occasion, appear on only one of those pages.

Index

Science and Religion

RELIGION IN AMERICA
A Very Short Introduction
Timothy Beal

Timothy Beal describes many aspects of religion in contemporary America that are typically ignored in other books on the subject, including religion in popular culture and counter-cultural groups; the growing phenomenon of "hybrid" religious identities, both individual and collective; the expanding numbers of new religious movements, or NRMs, in America; and interesting examples of "outsider religion." He also offers an engaging overview of the history of religion in America, from Native American traditions to the present day. Finally, Beal highlights the three major forces shaping the present and future of religion in America.

www.oup.com/vsi

Scientific Revolution
A Very Short Introduction
Lawrence M. Principe

In this *Very Short Introduction* Lawrence M. Principe explores the exciting developments in the sciences of the stars (astronomy, astrology, and cosmology), the sciences of earth (geography, geology, hydraulics, pneumatics), the sciences of matter and motion (alchemy, chemistry, kinematics, physics), the sciences of life (medicine, anatomy, biology, zoology), and much more. The story is told from the perspective of the historical characters themselves, emphasizing their background, context, reasoning, and motivations, and dispelling well-worn myths about the history of science.

www.oup.com/vsi

CATHOLICISM
A Very Short Introduction
Gerald O'Collins

Despite a long history of external threats and internal strife, the Roman Catholic Church and the broader reality of Catholicism remain a vast and valuable presence into the third millennium of world history. What are the origins of the Catholic Church? How has Catholicism changed and adapted to such vast and diverse cultural influences over the centuries? What great challenges does the Catholic Church now face in the twenty-first century, both within its own life and in its relation to others around the world? In this Very Short Introduction, Gerald O'Collins draws on the best current scholarship available to answer these questions and to present, in clear and accessible language, a fresh introduction to the largest and oldest institution in the world.

PENTECOSTALISM
A Very Short Introduction
William K. Kay

In religious terms Pentecostalism was probably the most vibrant and rapidly-growing religious movement of the 20th century. Starting as a revivalistic and renewal movement within Christianity, it encircled the globe in less than 25 years and grew in North America and then in those parts of the world with the highest birth-rates. Characterised by speaking in tongues, miracles, television evangelism and megachurches, it is also noted for its small-group meetings, empowerment of individuals, liberation of women and humanitarian concerns. William K Kay outlines the origins and growth of Pentecostalism, looking at not only the theological aspects of the movement, but also the sociological influences of its political and humanitarian viewpoints.

www.oup.com/vsi

PAGANISM
A Very Short Introduction
Owen Davies

This *Very Short Introduction* explores the meaning of paganism - through a chronological overview of the attitudes towards its practices and beliefs - from the ancient world through to the present day. Owen Davies largely looks at paganism through the eyes of the Christian world, and how, over the centuries, notions and representations of its nature were shaped by religious conflict, power struggles, colonialism, and scholarship. Despite the expansion of Christianity and Islam, Pagan cultures continue to exist around the world, whilst in the West new formations of paganism constitute one of the fastest-growing religions.

THE REFORMATION
A Very Short Introduction
Peter Marshall

The Reformation transformed Europe, and left an indelible mark on the modern world. It began as an argument about what Christians needed to do to be saved, but rapidly engulfed society in a series of fundamental changes. This *Very Short Introduction* provides a lively and up-to-date guide to the process. Peter Marshall argues that the Reformation was not a solely European phenomenon, but that varieties of faith exported from Europe transformed Christianity into a truly world religion. It explains doctrinal debates in a clear and non-technical way, but is equally concerned to demonstrate the effects the Reformation had on politics, society, art, and minorities.

www.oup.com/vsi